Judy Haning

Bridge of Love

GW00630877

Prayer Handbook
Advent 2002-2003

Contributors
   Brian Hudson, Terry Oakley,
   Rachel Poolman, Moira Rose,
   Alan Sayles, Heather Whyte.

Editor
   Norman Hart

Foreword

Bridges have been built at opposite ends of England to mark the beginning of the third millennium after the birth of Christ. One, across the Thames in London, has already become famous for the wrong reasons. It had to be closed immediately after its royal opening because it wobbled too much. When finally, in 2002, it had been stabilised, hundreds of people were invited to tramp across it together to demonstrate its bridgeworthiness. I suspect many of them took some delight in trying to make it wobble.

Another millennium bridge was built across the Tyne at Newcastle or, to give it its correct title, at Gateshead, south of the river, which is busy enlarging its attractions to match its big brother on the north shore. The London millennium bridge is attractive, even in its reinforced form. The Gateshead bridge, however is a thing of beauty, a pair of arches set at a right angle, one of which is the curved walkway which rises above the river to allow the passage of a boat. The arch in the illustration on the cover of this prayer handbook is the counterweight, which curves gracefully above the river at all times - a compressed rainbow which at first changed at night through a sequence of pastel coloured light beams.

I don't know what happens in London, but in Gateshead (and in Newcastle) people walk down to the river at night, even in the rain, just to gaze at the delicate arc amid the monster cranes and the massive spans of the familiar road and rail bridges. It was this bridge which came to my mind when the committee seeking a name for this handbook were seized by the title Bridge of Love, which Heather Whyte had given to her prayer for April 27, with an echo in the rainbow prayer written by Moira Rose for March 9.

The Bridge of Love is Jesus Christ, who has 'crossed the chasm between God and the world' and links us to God and to one another (April 27). It is the bridge 'between despair and hope' upon which many who have not yet seen it will one day step 'and feel the power surge through them'. It is the rainbow which God set in the sky as a promise to all creation that his grace still shines (March 9).

It is also prayer itself, which links us to Father, Son and Holy Spirit in confession and petititon, intercession and praise. Just occasionally we feel our prayers soaring beautifully, like Gateshead's shining arch, lifting us above the river of our rushing lives and lighting up the night of pain and incomprehension in which our world too often lives. More often I can see prayer in the black and white photograph of the half-completed Tyne road bridge which I have in a book of Tyneside memories. The two suspended halves of the incomplete span reach towards each other from opposite shores of the river. My father-in-law, whose book it was, was taken as a schoolboy to watch the spans on the day they joined.

For most of us prayer has to be built in the same way. God is there, reaching out to us, listening, ready to answer. We have to build the other half-span to reach him. We hope this book will help.

Again this year we have six writers:
Brian Hudson was a member and worship leader at Leaside URC/Methodist Church in Ware, now living in Ledbury; *Terry Oakley* is Development Strategy Officer for URC Northern Synod, working with local churches, District Councils and the Synod on strategies for mission and development; *Rachel Poolman* is a minister, who as the current holder of the URC Research Scholarship is preparing a thesis on 'Understandings of Worship in the URC'; *Moira Rose* is a primary school teacher, and elder and worship leader at Carver URC in Windermere; *Alan Sayles* is local leader and elder of Writtle URC and part-time almshouse administrator; *Heather Whyte* is in her final year of training for ministry, on internship placement at Abington Avenue URC, Northampton.

They have tried to offer prayers which can be used in public worship as well as private devotion, together with some meditations. Their sources have been the Scripture passages set for each Sunday and some other holy days in the Revised Common Lectionary, passages which are listed at the top of each prayer page. Where inspiration has come from one or two particular passages they are repeated above the prayer itself.

On the facing pages there are glimpses of the life of the Council for World Mission's 31 member Churches around the world, to illustrate the requests for prayer found in the central pages of the handbook.

They are arranged more or less in the order in which these countries appear in the World Council of Churches ecumenical prayer cycle. There are also references to special Sundays or special weeks observed by a variety of groups who pray.

The bridge of prayer has many spans.

I would like to have used more topical material about the hard questions people are struggling with around the world; but their situations change dramatically from one night's television news to the next, leaving behind the weekly news magazines let alone an annual prayer handbook. The rainbow bridge does draw attention to one people's current questions, however. Ten thousand Tuvaluan Christians believe strongly in God's covenant with Noah that he will never flood the earth again. Man's wisdom says that Tuvalu will on some not too distant day be covered by the rising seas. How should we pray for Tuvalu?

Norman Hart

Seven Ages for Prayer

Ideas for meditation and prayer based on Jaques' speech in Shakespeare's *As You Like It*, Act II, scene 7, often called The Seven Ages of Man.

THE FIRST AGE
At first the infant, mewling and puking in the nurse's arms
Something of the attractiveness of very young babies lies in their helplessness. People with no reason to harbour maternal instincts still feel the need to shelter, support, pacify, comfort the youngest children. The infant Jesus makes his first appeal at Christmastime by his human helplessness, even before it is contrasted with his divinity and his destiny. *'Hark, hark, the wise eternal Word as a weak infant cries.'* We may pray for good health, strength and intelligence for our own children, our grandchildren and our godchildren, but all infants need protective prayers. If they are helpless in all times and places, fighting and famine place them in the greatest need. The father of an unborn child was shot dead early in 2002 while driving his wife to the hospital delivery room through a military checkpoint. Pray for infants you know or learn about who begin life orphaned, in deep poverty or hostile surroundings. Because tiny children cannot help themselves, pray for parents, midwives and doctors, neighbours and all who seek to give them safe passage into a dangerous world. Pray for those baptised, dedicated or blessed in your church.

THE SECOND AGE
The whining schoolboy, with his satchel and shining morning face, creeping like snail unwillingly to school
Shakespeare's Jaques described a schoolboy still recognisable today, but thousands of children go to school gladly and thousands more long to be able to go. Pray for those who devise our educational systems and those who teach in them, and pray for the children whose minds and characters are shaped by them. The Latin word 'educo' means the drawing out of the child's God-given gifts and abilities through good teaching. Pray that our children may take advantage of the best that is offered them, with our own encouragement.

Pray for children the world over for whom there are not enough schools, or teachers, or whose poverty denies them any chance of formal education. Pray for girls refused education because they are girls. Pray for those who teach and nurture children in our churches. Pray that parents may recognise the teaching that takes place, consciously or unconsciously, in every home, so that Christian character may grow in step with knowledge. Think especially of children and families known to you; in your church.

THE THIRD AGE

The lover, sighing like a furnace, with a woeful ballad made to his mistress' eyebrow

Our hormones are also God-given, often arousing in us that particular kind of love which leads to partnership, marriage, the making of a family. First love is sometimes painful, embarrassing even, and yet so demanding that it rearranges a young person's life. Today male and female attractiveness fuel sales campaigns, and the noble emotion of love for another person is often disfigured by easy promiscuity. Pray for young people who, in every society, are looking for true love - and being sold cheap substitutes. Pray for those seeking excitement from drugs. Pray for parents, who so often feel distanced from their children at this stage of life, and for all who have the opportunity of counselling and supporting young adults - friends, teachers, ministers, youth workers. Sex education can be taught in class but love cannot.

In our society learning and earning now preoccupy not just the 20-somethings but also the 30-somethings. For many the desire for partnership and home-making compete with career demands. Pray for young people you know who are facing these years in a variety of ways. Pray for those in your church (or those who were until recently in your church).

THE FOURTH AGE

Then a soldier, full of strange oaths and bearded like the pard

It's not a bad idea to pray for soldiers, or for all servicemen and women, when all around the world wars are being considered, or fought, or, just occasionally, ended. Pray for conscript troops, for those fighting for their own lives and the lives of their families, for mercenaries, for peacekeeping forces, for service chaplains and for our own country's troops, in barracks or on active service. But the soldier here stands for all working men and women at the peak of their powers. Some of them, like Shakespeare's soldier, are seeking 'the bubble reputation'; some are doing the work they have chosen and trained for; some are working to feed and clothe themselves and their families, to maintain a home and pay the mortgage. Think through the congregation that you know best and pray as best your knowledge of these working people allows. As the years of education are extended and the health and medical treatment of those in retirement gives them a longer lifespan, a smaller proportion of the population than ever before is working to support our sophisticated community services. Pray for those who regulate wages and taxes, that every worker's contribution may be respected and rewarded. Pray for those without work and those disabled in the prime of their working life. The parable of the labourers in the vineyard *(Matthew 20)* reminds us of God's concern for the needs of every person.

THE FIFTH AGE

The justice... full of wise saws and moral instances, and so he plays his part

Judges and lawmakers are our rule-makers and moderators, sharing with governments and elected members of parliamentary assemblies in the task of creating a just society for us all. With them, in our prayers, we may include a wide range of 'professional' people - in the legal and medical professions, the civil service, directors of businesses, the teaching profession from pre-school to university, the police and the social services. It is here that we sometimes observe the widest gaps in the fabric of society: men and women out of touch with those they are supposed to represent; lawmaking which is ignorant of the actual effect of the law on people's lives; huge differences in income without any obvious justification in the intensity and quality of the work done. Pray for these 'professional' people as you know of them or about them. Pray for justice, and caring, and commitment in our society, and since praying for abstract things is very difficult, look for events or people on which you can focus your prayers - a court case, a local hero, a parliamentary debate. The 'wise saws and moral instances' of Shakespeare's Justice may have been mentioned with irony, but we need the part they play in our lives.

THE SIXTH AGE

shifts into the lean and slippered pantaloon, with spectacles on nose
The last two of Shakespeare's Seven Ages are of people in decline, and perhaps we can claim today to have slowed down the descent into oblivion, even if we have been using spectacles for many years. One who would have been a 'lean and slippered pantaloon' is often today engaged in an active retirement, a voluntary worker whose skills benefit the community as much as they did when he or she worked for money. Give thanks for older people with the willingness, wit and energy to fill the gaps in society, whether as hospital drivers, workers for charities, church and community visitors, lay preachers, babysitters for their grandchildren or leaders in the University of the Third Age. Pray for them and for those you know whose failing health does not allow them to continue to contribute in this way, who have had to accept slippers in place of outdoor shoes. Many of them have the time and the wisdom to maintain a ministry of prayer while sitting at home.
Pray for those who can no longer look after themselves and now share a communal home. Pray for relatives who cannot find time to visit and listen to people living in the quiet byroads of society, for carers looking after the older generation in their own homes, for elderly people caring for partners, whose own strength may not be up to the task to which they have devoted themselves. Pray for those made prematurely dependent on others; those coping with life-changing illness, with sudden loss of a faculty - sight or hearing, or those with Alzheimer's disease.

THE SEVENTH AGE

Last scene of all is ...second childishness and mere oblivion
Pray for those whose life has extended beyond the lives of those they loved; those who would be happy to accept childishness and oblivion to what is happening around them in exchange for the emptiness they feel. Pray that God's embrace may be near to those who face death, those who fear it and those who long for it to come. Pray for those who work in hospices and among the terminally ill.
Pray for yourself, that in all your needs you will find God at your side.

Isaiah 64:1-9
Psalm 80:1-7, 17-19
1 Corinthians 1:3-9
Mark 13:24-37

Fighting AIDS

In 2001, of the estimated 36 million people worldwide living with HIV, 25 million were in southern and central Africa. Already 16 million Africans had died of AIDS. But while governments were slow to acknowledge the ravages of the virus among their people, sufferers in many countries were fighting a positive battle to turn back the disease.

Uganda is unique among sub-Saharan African countries in that the rate of HIV infection is falling. The government and churches have spoken openly about the crisis, its causes and the ways HIV/AIDS can be combatted. Church of Uganda minister Gideon Byamugisha was the first priest in Africa to state that he was living with HIV. When he decided to tell his bishop that he was HIV positive he expected 'to be thrown out'. Instead his bishop knelt and prayed for him and told him that he had a special mission in the Church. Now Health Secretary for the Diocese of Namirembe, Mr Byamugisha speaks of the surprise he encounters when people see him buying condoms in local shops. He explains, 'I am a person living with HIV and I am married. That's why I need to buy condoms.'

In South Africa, members of the Treatment Action Campaign in Durban took part in a march during the AIDS Conference in Durban in 2000, to give the lie to the image of powerless people waiting for death. The chair of the Campaign, Zachie Achmat, has chosen not to take retroviral medication himself until it is available to everyone in South Africa who needs it.

In Zambia, where AIDS has killed at least 650,000 people in the 18 years since it was first recorded, and orphaned some 800,000 children, respected former President Kenneth Kaunda this year took a public HIV test and challenged the country's top politicians to do the same. Found to be HIV-negative, he urged all Zambians to take the test 'because this is the only way that will help us to fight the disease.'

Come down

Read   Isaiah 64:1-9

✓ *Come down, O Lord, and make your name known to your enemies.*

     Come down, Lord, and set the world to rights.
     Come down and show yourself to those who deny you,
     Come down and cause the nations to quake.

     But you came down, Lord, and we did not recognise you.

✓ *Come down, O Lord, that we may be saved.*

     Come down, that we may see your face, shining on us,
         restoring us.
     Come down, then we will not turn away from you.

     But you came down, Lord, and we did turn away.

✓ *Come again, O Lord, to save us.*

     In your own time, come again to gather your people to yourself,
         to complete your eternal purpose,
         to bring about the final triumph of your holy kingdom.

     But we acknowledge, Lord, that we need to prepare
         ourselves for that great day.

✓ So come again, Lord;
✓ in this season of Advent, come into our hearts
✓ so that, like kindling on a fire, we burst into flame,
✓   and, like boiling water, bubble with joy;
✓ and, as we eagerly await your return,
     may we turn towards you,
     may we be restored,
✓   may we recognise you as Lord, Creator, Judge of all,
         and as our loving, forgiving Father.

Ploughshares

Transforming Arms into Ploughshares, a church-run programme to recycle the legacy of Mozambique's 16-year civil war, has collected and destroyed more than 200,000 guns, grenades and rocket-launchers which were among millions of weapons hidden in the country at the time of the peace agreement in 1992. The arms have been exchanged for farm tools, sewing machines, hoes and bicycles. Artists have created works of art from the decommissioned weapons, making them into human forms, models of animals and birds, musical instruments and chairs, and these have been sold to support the project. Christian Aid put many of them on display in London early in 2002.

Pray with Mozambique synod of the United Congregational Church in Southern Africa (CWM Africa region).

The Christian contribution to nation-building, the Christian vision for India and the Church as a pro-active channel of truth, peace and justice are the themes of an ecumenical Christian Festival - Masih Mahotsav - being held in India at the beginning of this month. Agreed by the representatives of Catholic, Evangelical, Orthodox and Protestant church bodies in India, which include three CWM member churches, the festival will invite over 3,000 prominent Christians as a show of solidarity on behalf of the 25 million Christians in the nation. It ends with a massive convention of Christians from all over the country in New Delhi.

He's coming

Read   Isaiah 40:9; 2 Peter 3:13

He's coming! Rejoice!

> Give thanks. Hallelujah!
> Sins forgiven. Salvation is near.
> He is gathering us into his arms.
>
> He's coming! Give thanks and rejoice.

He's coming! Prepare!

> Don't be caught out.
> A new heaven. A new earth.
> Don't be found living in the old way.
>
> He's coming! Give thanks and prepare.

He's coming! You know it!

> You've heard his messengers.
> You can feel it in the air.
> Don't keep it to yourself! Lift up your voice and shout!
>
> He's coming! Hallelujah!

Thanks be to God.

Near death

A letter to a URC member in Walton-on-Thames, England, from the URC's Commitment for Life partner in Zimbabwe, reports:
'I picked up a young man who had collapsed along the road. I suspect he had a bad attack of malaria. He did not have the money to go to the clinic and could not afford to buy a course of Chloroquin for 20 pence, and he would very likely have died without the tablets... People literally die in front of locked gates of the hospitals. In the midst of all this bad news, people keep their wonderful smiles and even joke...'

The Revd Farai Chirisa, a former bishop of the Methodist Church in Zimbabwe, prays:
Lord God, we give you thanks for sending your only Son to give us life. We thank you for our country, Zimbabwe, and its rich human and natural resources. Yet in the midst of wealth we are crushed by poverty, and while we are offered Christ's life in all its fullness, we are ever surrounded by disease, death and destruction. We are tempted by despair, and yet keep hoping, knowing that you care. At times we weep silent tears and cry out with deep emotion. We come to you, our only hope and refuge. Thank you for the gift of laughter, even when the going is tough. With you, O Lord, we may be troubled but not destroyed.

Pray with Zimbabwe synod of the United Congregational Church in Southern Africa and with Zimbabwe presbytery of the Uniting Presbyterian Church in Southern Africa (CWM Africa region).

Read **John 1:6-8; 1 Thessalonians 5:16-24**

Lord God, you have sent your messengers
>to remind us of your continuing presence with your people,
>to inspire us when our vision becomes blurred,
to call us back to a right way of living.

>Lord, we hear your words with joy
>**And praise you with all our being.**

Lord God, your messengers bring new hope
>to those imprisoned by the burdens of daily living,
>to those whose tears block out the sunlight,
>to those hungry for a new world and a new relationship with you.

>Lord, we hear your words with joy
>**And praise you with all our being.**

Lord God, your messengers bring new joy
>for you have filled our barrenness with your life giving spirit,
>you have replaced our weakness with your strength,
>you have called all humanity to be your holy people
>>and to know the salvation that is available to everyone.

>Lord, we hear your words with joy
>**And praise you with all our being.**

>**Thanks be to God.**

Non-violent

Churches in Namibia have called for the government and people of the country to work to overcome violence and cultivate peace. Saying that people across the country now live in fear of violent robbery, the Council of Churches in Namibia has pledged to educate the people in its member churches in the ways of non-violence through sermons and meetings and in children's education. It is urging local communities to cooperate in building a world of peace by opposing the perpetrators and instruments of violence and upholding the value and dignity of life. The Council promotes marriage enrichment programmes, and has also committed itself to promote the rights of women and disabled people within the churches and to raise awareness of the effects of alcohol and drug abuse.

Pray with Namibia synod of the Congregational Church in Southern Africa (CWM Africa region).

God in a box

Read   2 Samuel 7:1-11; Luke 1:26-38

King David said to the prophet Nathan: "Here am I living in a house
built of cedar, but God's covenant box is kept in a tent!"

An easy mistake to make.
Any one of us might have done the same.

'God is in the box – and even that's only in a tent.
Let's build a bigger house for him
    or a better church or a bigger cathedral.'

But, says God, I don't live in a box.
I am living in the lives of my people.

Lord, we try to keep you locked up in boxes of our own making –
    boxes of tradition, of familiar words, of people and places we know.
But you are not to be confined by bricks and mortar, nor by our narrow
vision.
Forgive us when we try to wrap you up like a Christmas present that
we keep to ourselves,
    for you are a God for all peoples, all times and all places.

Lord, you have the habit of jumping out of the box when we least
expect it.
You catch us unprepared, just as you surprised Mary with the glorious
news of Christ's coming.
And still you say to us: I have a task for you – nothing is impossible
with God.
Teach us, with Mary, to reply: May it be as you have said.

Lord, jump out of the box in which we have tried to imprison you:
The incredible Christmas news is for all nations.

Open wide the closed doors of our minds
And take us where you will.

Landless

Southern African governments have been urged by the United Congregational Church in Southern Africa (UCCSA) to safeguard people's God-given right to own land and to address the problem of landlessness. It has called on governments and political parties to use legal and just means when reallocating land, with the interests both of landowners and the landless taken into consideration.. 'This is of particular significance in the light of the land invasions in Zimbabwe and certain politically-inspired land occupations in isolated parts of South Africa,' says UCCSA media officer Dave Wanless.

Both the United Congregational and the Uniting Presbyterian Churches in Southern Africa regularly find themselves dealing with refugee and immigrant concerns. Local churches are often more closely involved with the issue than national church bodies, especially churches on the borders with other states. Mining regions, which draw in people looking for jobs, are a particular concern. 'Ours is the church for the stranger,' says the Revd White Rakuba of the South African Council of Churches. Christianity remains, properly, above restrictive nationalisms and patriotisms.

Pray with the South African presbytery of the Uniting Presbyterian Church and the South African synod of the United Congregational Church in Southern Africa (CWM Africa region).

Come Lord Jesus – the time is right.

In the peace of a darkened night,
In the beauty of the leafless trees against a winter moon,
In the quietness of a hallowed church,

come Lord Jesus – the time is right.

In the neon glare of a city's artificial day,
In the squalor of Cardboard City or the rubbish dump where street children live,
In the noise of the party and revelry,

come Lord Jesus – the time is right.

In the joy of a waiting heart,
In the excitement of half asleep children,
In the gathering of your holy people,

come Lord Jesus – the time is right.

In the pain of an aching heart,
In the cries of an abused child,
In the loneliness of those who have no one,

come Lord Jesus – the time is right.

In the stillness of my mind,
In the love of my heart,
In the skills of my hand,

come Lord Jesus – the time is indeed right.
I pray you will find me ready.

Nativity play   *Lights, camels, action*

It could be the pantomime.

The set is a village street – a line of shop-fronts and the village inn, where the women's chorus are making the beds. Centre-stage there is, surprisingly, a cowshed with an ox and a donkey. Are they real, or people in pantomime suits?
Within the cowshed are the principal girl, and the principal ... man, standing firmly by her. The principal girl has a baby, a new-born baby. Enter, stage left, the men's chorus, dressed as shepherds and carrying lambs, real lambs.

In Act Two, after an interval, the magicians arrive. What costumes, what splendour of silk and gold, what a spectacle. The lighting is pretty good, too. Only a star – but such a star!
The magicians bring a surprise – mysterious presents for the baby, gift-wrapped. The heavenly orchestra, high above the stage, brings its music to a splendid crescendo as the gifts are presented, and the chorus bursts out singing.

Brilliant God, director and producer, we love our pantomime and we imagine you do too. When Boxing Day comes, anchor us in the reality of the life and death and rising of Jesus, our star.

Surprised?

Read Luke 2:1-14

Quiet and unnoticed, he's come into his world
No fanfare from the castle top, no banners were unfurled
No proclamation read aloud that here's your future king
For so very few the people who heard the angels sing
Just a handful on the hillside that came to watch and pray –
We shouldn't be surprised at that: it happens every day.

Quiet and unnoticed, he's resting on the straw
No rush from those inside the inn to find the stable door
There's food to cook, the clothes to wash, the rooms to clean
        and sweep
And so very few the people who see him there asleep.
Some come to see a baby and, as they watch, they pray –
We shouldn't be surprised at that: it happens every day.

Quiet and unnoticed, he's come to change our life
To offer hope for our despair, his peace instead of strife
His arms outstretched with love and tears, his birth is now, for all
But so very few the people who truly hear his call.
Some twist his words to suit their ends, let others watch and pray –
We shouldn't be surprised at that: it happens every day.

Quiet and unnoticed, God's sent his only son
No thunderbolts, no lightning flash announce what he's begun:
From Bethlehem to all the world, Christ Jesus comes to reign
As his sacrificial love unites us all with God again –
And countless lives are changed by love when people watch
        and pray –
We shouldn't be surprised at that: it happens every day.

Thankfulness

The conversion or influencing of the chiefs of Botswana by the early missionaries, white and black, created a Christian 'climate' which led to today's Republic of Botswana professing Christianity while enshrining religious freedom in its constitution. While no-one would claim that the African nation's life is perfect, the rule of law operates well in Botswana and there has never been any tampering with elections, which have been free and fair without fail every five years since independence. The dominance of one party in that time has not led to dictatorship. Botswana had no need of a liberation struggle; it has experienced no civil wars and has no political prisoners.

Though nowadays fragmented, the Christian Church is a significant element in the population and Christian values are reflected in legislation and the national life. Batswana give thanks to God for these facts of present-day life, which serve to balance the desperate image of Africa as a continent which is often the only one publicised.

Of course the country has causes of concern. Per head of the population, it has the highest incidence of AIDS infection in the world. The Government is using its diamond wealth to provide expensive retroviral drugs for sufferers and the churches are involved in counselling, orphanages and feeding schemes for adults and orphans.

Botswana also has a human rights problem with the San (or Bushmen). Recognised as the original inhabitants of the country, they enjoy full citizens' rights and many are involved in commerce and the professions. For the remnant who still practise hunting and gathering a reserve was created where they could live in the traditional way, but the Government has recently decided to relocate them in villages with facilities such as schools and clinics. The move has been fiercely criticised and both the San and the Government need people's prayers.

Pray with Botswana synod of the United Congregational Church in Southern Africa (CWM Africa region).

My child

My child, unique and special, you are not mine alone, but God's.
God names you.
My child, lovely and precious, you are not mine to own, but to endow.
God names you.
My child, delightful and fragile, you are not mine to hold, but to let go.
God names you.

This child

This child, presented to God, presents us with a crisis of choice.
God names us.
This child, destined by God, determines our future fortune.
God names us.
This child, favoured of God, fills us with prospects of peace.
God names us.

God's children

God's children are clothed in liberty and dressed in justice.
God's name be praised.
God's children are adopted as family and welcomed as friends.
God's name be praised.
God's children are filled with the Spirit and inherit God's name.
God's name be praised.

*(In worship, especially in a baptismal service or a service of
dedication, the first stanza may be said by the parents, the second
by the worship leader and the third by all the worshippers.)*

Regeneration

The community of Drumchapel was built in the 1950s on Glasgow's western boundary to house people working in local industries. Today it is a 'regeneration area', from which people are temporarily moved while new housing is built.

Drumchapel's churches have joined in the regeneration, with St Andrew's and St Mark's congregations of the Church of Scotland, the Episcopal and United Reformed churches and St Pius X Roman Catholic church covenanted together to share their common vision in Christ with the community. The Emmaus Family Project supported originally by one of the Roman Catholic congregations and itself a partner in the covenant, is a key element in the Drumchapel Churches Partnership. Based in two of the churches and in the shopping centre, its four staff welcome families, young mothers and children and run a range of activities to develop life skills.

In many other ways the partnership has raised the churches' profile, witnessing against sectarianism as Protestants and Catholics work and worship together, working with secular agencies and gaining a voice in the community not so much for themselves as for those who formerly were unheard.

Pray with the churches in Scotland.

Read   John 1:10-18

God, we dream how good it is going to be!

You will give us strong defences,
beautiful children, peaceful borders
and finest food.

You will melt the snow,
set the wind at our back, turn the tide for us,
put the law on our side.

You will gather us
from the north and south, easing the way
for disabled and pregnant.

You will bring us with tears of relief
to stroll along the stream,
by the smooth straight path.

You will be our father,
our shepherd, our rescuer, our provider
of food and wine

You will make life like a bed of roses,
the young men will make merry
and the damsels will dance.

...

God, we wake up to the reality that
those who knew, those who welcomed,
those who believed when you came,
were empowered to become Children of God.

Strangers

Over the past ten years the gap between rich and poor in Hong Kong has increased, and the number of immigrants from Indonesia has grown from 1.2 to 2.1 percent of the population, according to the latest census. The figures show new areas in which the Church must carry out its mission, says the Revd Eric So, general secretary of Hong Kong Christian Council. 'As the Church, we must also consider the new arrivals from mainland China. For example, we should consider what kind of message is appropriate and meaningful to those coming from a socialist and traditional society. While some churches are very eager to sponsor overseas evangelism, we must think about the Christian mission for the strangers among us in Hong Kong.'

Pray with the Hong Kong Council of the Church of Christ in China (CWM East Asia region).

Epiphany of the Lord

God, isn't it amazing?
The wise had to ask …
the strangers came to pay tribute …
the king was frightened …
> where the Messiah was born.

God, isn't it strange?
The astrologers found in the stars …
the foreigners brought their wealth …
the king was not to be trusted …
> when the Messiah was born.

God, isn't it mysterious?
The persecutor becomes the prisoner …
the least reaches the most …
the suffering of the King reveals the glory …
> because the Messiah was born.

God, isn't it obvious?
The truth is plain to see …
it's as clear as daylight …
the true King was delivering the needy …
> as the Messiah was born.

Epiphany 1
Baptism of the Lord

Read   **Genesis 1:1-5; Mark 1:4-11**

Within creation
formless darkness is not enough.
So the voice said 'Light'
and separated day and night.
And God is satisfied.
Bless us with your light.

Within creation
thundering water is not enough.
So in heaven voices say 'Glory'
and on earth voices cry 'Glory'.
And God is proclaimed.
Bless us with your glory.

Within Church
Repentance is not enough.
So a wilderness voice says 'Baptise'
and sins are forgiven.
And God is pleased.
Bless us with your forgiveness.

Within Church
baptism by water is not enough.
So an apostle's voice says 'Jesus'
and the Holy Spirit is received.
And God is praised.
Bless us with your Spirit.

In Britain this is the Week of Prayer for Christian Unity.

Shore-love

Deep sea fishermen who work out of Kaohsiung harbour, Taiwan,
sometimes spend as much as three years away from home.
Every year from September to late November some of the larger
boats are in the port and their crews get a little shore leave.
So the Seamen's and Fishermen's Service Centre, a ministry of the
Presbyterian Church in Taiwan has begun holding an early Christmas
party for crews returning from the South Atlantic fishing grounds.
Last year's party was held on November 18 for 40 seamen, mostly
Filipinos. Most of the foreign crew members on Taiwanese-owned
fishing vessels are from the Philippines - low-paid and far from home.
'Our purpose is to provide a bit of family feeling,' says Centre director
John Chou, 'and to share the love of Christ.'

Pray with the Presbyterian Church in Taiwan (CWM East Asia region).

Read   1 Samuel 3:1-20

God, I confess
I hear your Word
revealing your
knowledge of me
and I am ashamed
of my faults and failings.

God, I confess
I hear your Word
challenging my
knowledge of sin
and I am ashamed
of my body's betrayal.

God, I confess
I hear your Word
praising my
knowledge of truth
and I am ashamed
of my tentative trust.

God, I profess.
I speak your Word
telling my
knowledge of you
and I am glad
of knowing you knowing me.

Marginalised

The Presbyterian Church in the Republic of Korea (PROK) has set up six 'House of a New Tomorrow' centres to help unemployed people, providing free meals, counselling and job information. The PROK also has 30 churches for the country's marginalised people - the Minjung - a title which includes disabled people, farmers, the elderly, orphans, undocumented migrant workers, homeless teenagers and sex workers. The churches have food and educational programmes for the unemployed and homeless, with the help of CWM sponsorship in funding the work and providing staff training.

Pray with the Presbyterian Church in the Republic of Korea (CWM East Asia region).

Read   Jonah 3:1-5,10

In times long past
people hoped for change
from their rock and refuge -
for God to change
the powers…
Empower us, God.

In less than forty days
the city changed
from its feasting to fasting
so God changed
from anger…
Forgive us, God.

In less time than that
the world will change
from present to passing
but will we change
our attachments…?
Release us, God.

Now is the time
for me to change
from fear to faith
as I change
to follow…
Call us, God.

Gospel cakes

A congregation of the Gereja Presbyterian Malaysia is reaching out to its Chinese community by using Chinese festivals to share the Christian faith. The Mooncake festival takes place every summer, with Chinese people baking and eating small round cakes. Hebron Presbyterian Church in Johore Bahru, a Chinese congregation, makes cakes with gospel messages inside and distributes them to Buddhist Chinese. At the Chinese New Year, when church members hand out oranges, a traditional gift, they start conversations with local people about the Christian faith. Hebron church deacon Michael Tay says, 'It's to let them know that we're Chinese too, and we want to bless them. It's also to let them know who and where we are, so that they can come to evangelistic meetings.'

Pray with Gereja Presbyterian Malaysia (CWM East Asia region).

Pray for the staff of the Council for World Mission, who service its programmes, its funding and its decision-making. CWM is a community of 31 mainline Protestant churches worldwide, committed to sharing their resources of money, people, skills and insights globally to carry out God's mission locally.

Read   I Corinthians 8:1-13

O God, source of all wisdom,
you made a world of difference.
People far away and close to home
are each made in your image,
but are rarely of one mind.

Give us sensitivity to those we meet
that we may listen to their stories
and understand their journeys.

Forgive us when we are puffed up by knowledge
and think we are above actions
that will build others up in love.
Free us from our desire to be right
and turn us towards the truths that others see.

O God, source of all wisdom,
thank you for the gift of life
and for our world of difference.

With your help we will live life well
and grow together
beyond our differences.

Bridge work

Rifts between house churches and the state-recognised church in China are being bridged by the Presbyterian Church in Singapore. The Three-Self Patriotic Movement, the government-sanctioned Protestant church, maintains that the booming house church movement is causing problems for Christians by refusing to gain state approval. The house churches accuse the recognised church of putting the state before the Bible.

The Presbyterian Church in Singapore has links with both parts of the Chinese church. The congregation in which Presbyterian moderator the Revd Tan Cheng Hock ministers sends a group to visit local Three Self congregations and another to the house churches and tries to heal their divisions. Leaders of both churches come to Singapore to train - Three Self leaders to Trinity Theological College and house church leaders to Singapore Bible College. The latter cannot be persuaded to train at Trinity because they say Three Self leaders there will spy on them and report them to the authorities in China.

Pray with the Presbyterian Church in Singapore (CWM East Asia region).

Read   Isaiah 40:21-31

God of the universe,
You oversee the earth and its unfolding events;
You inhabit all time and dwell in people's hearts.

You sit above the circle of the earth;
We reach to you, creating God.

The world changes and confronts us with the unexpected
but you are one with us
and cannot let us go.

Your understanding is unsearchable.
We open our heart to you, nurturing God.

Your work is eternal,
your truth is magnificent,
your passion unspent.

You strengthen the powerless.
We trust in you, soul-searching God.

You invite us
to rise up with wings like eagles,
to run and not be weary,
to walk and not grow faint.

You will renew our strength.
We worship you, life-changing God.

16 February
Education Sunday

2 Kings 5:1-14
Psalm 30
1 Corinthians 9:24-27
Mark 1 40-45

Struggling to learn

The Eastern Cape Province, South Africa's poorest, spends nearly all its education budget on the salaries of teachers and administrators. Most schools that I visited had received no textbooks since 1997, despite the introduction of a new syllabus. There was no money for repairs - a coloured school where three classrooms were burnt down by vandals from outside the school was told that their repair was 'a community responsibility'. Another black school was putting up with 'temporary' classrooms of uninsulated zinc built fifteen years ago - boiling hot in summer, freezing cold in winter - with no prospect of any new buildings.

Few black schools have adequately equipped science laboratories, and in some cases children take exams in physical science or biology without having been able to conduct or witness any of the necessary experiments or models. Subject choices are limited and the minimal pass rate in maths deters most black children from taking it - many opting instead for Afrikaans, often the only alternative but a far less useful qualification.

South Africa is not short of teachers, but it is desperately short of good ones. I was therefore appalled to hear that Britain had been seeking to recruit teachers in South Africa to alleviate its own shortages.

Tony Lemon
in 'Mansfield College Record'

When we are living in the night-time
and do not know if there is a way ahead;
when the ordinariness of life is dull
and our daily load is heavy;
when we believe that the dawn is breaking
but are wary of what the light might reveal:

Help us to know that by your presence you proclaim:
**Weeping may linger for the night
        but joy comes with the morning.**

For those who cannot escape the darkness
and are untouchable in their pain;
for those whose troubles seem routine
and who keep going, saying little;
for those whose lives are full,
who worry what will happen if just one thing goes wrong.

Help us through our presence to proclaim:
**Weeping may linger for the night
        but joy comes with the morning.**

When nations and peoples are trapped
in the long dark night of war and conflict;
when the struggle to live lasts a lifetime cut short,
when disease or disaster destroys fragile hope:

Let us not be glib when we proclaim:
**Weeping may linger for the night
        but joy comes with the morning.**

Let us point to the Christ who wept,
the Christ who was shrouded in darkness,
the Christ who lives beyond the night,
the Christ who walks with us,
to the joy that will come in the morning.

Global morality

At the end of an increasingly secular century, it has been the biblical proof and moral imagination of religion that have torched the principles of the hitherto unassailable citadels of international finance -and opened the way to a radicalism about capitalism whose ramifications are not yet understood. There is the moral basis for a new social settlement. The Left of Centre should take note: it is no longer Morris, Keynes and Beveridge who inspire and change the world - it's Leviticus.   *Will Hutton*

I started talking about Third World debt because it was clear that people in Britain do not die of drought, people in the mid-West of America do not die of drought, so why do they die of drought in Africa? They do not. They are dying of politics.   *Bob Geldof*

The poverty in our century is unlike that of any other. It is not, as poverty was before, the result of natural scarcity, but of a set of priorities imposed upon the rest of the world by the rich. Consequently, the modern poor are not pitied but written off as trash. The twentieth century consumer economy has produced the first culture for which a beggar is a reminder of nothing.   *John Berger*

Read Isaiah 43:18-25

God, you promise to do a new thing,
to transform the wilderness,
to gather up all creation to join in an endless hymn of praise;

And here we are again,
gathered together to offer you our worship.
Our lives don't feel so very different from yesterday.
We are not expecting big changes by next week.
We want to be here with you and with each other
but we might be surprised if you did a new thing.

Shake us from our torpor,
from our addiction to the predictable and expected.
Free us to open our hearts and minds
to new gifts blossoming unnoticed,
to life springing forth all around us.

Forgive us for our preoccupation with ourselves
and with what we want from you.
Help us to recognise what we can give to you
in our worship and in our lives.

God of the ages, who makes all things new,
we offer you our praise, our thanksgiving,
our worship, our hearts and our lives.

Glory be to you O God.

A job worth doing

Some 40 Jobcentres in England were visited towards the end of 2000 by members of local United Reformed churches, not in search of work but to collect data for a survey of the type and quality of jobs on offer in the centres. They found that nearly 39% of the jobs were part-time and over 14% were temporary or casual and not offering an effective route back to work for unemployed people. More than a fifth of the vacancies did not pay enough for the worker to qualify for National Insurance sick or maternity pay benefits, contributory Jobseekers Allowance or a state pension. More than half the jobs paid less than a couple with two children under 11 would get on Income Support.

In an introduction to the findings, URC General Secretary David Cornick says that the reason why the Church should be concerned about unemployment and the distribution of jobs in society is that God's love is a just love. Christians need to challenge 'unjust' structures in society. 'The quality of a civilisation can be judged by its treatment of the poor.'

The challenge to Christians, says URC Church and Society Secretary Andrew Bradstock, is how they can continue to align themselves with those who have suffered from poverty and unemployment over the years, and ensure that they are not pushed into poor quality jobs.

Pray with the United Reformed Church (in Britain - CWM Europe region).

All we are asked to do

Read 2 Kings 2:1-12; 2 Corinthians 4:3-6; Mark 9:2-9

Elisha sees Elijah disappearing in a chariot of fire,
receives a double share of his spirit
and picks up his mantle.

Peter, James and John stand on a mountain top,
see Jesus transfigured
and are entrusted with the truth.

The mantle has been passed on,
the sacred truth inherited
by us,
Christ's followers,
in this world, in this time.

The mantle does not feel comfortable;
the truth leaves us dumbstruck;
looking into the light is hard.

And yet the mantle is ours,
the truth still lives,
the light still shines.

Christ calls us
to proclaim the truth and reflect the light
through the choices we make,
the way we love
and the risks we take.

All we are asked to do is wear the mantle,
receive our inheritance
and walk towards the light.

*For it is the God who has said 'let light shine out of darkness'
who has shone in our hearts to give the light of the knowledge
of the glory of God in the face of Jesus Christ.*

Rwanda's refugees

After the riots of 1959, thousands of Tutsi fled to Burundi, Uganda, Tanzania and Zaire. In their minds this was just a temporary migration. It lasted 30 years. Here and there along the borders there were attempts to negotiate the return of the refugees. But extremists on both sides opposed them. Inside Rwanda, people had appropriated property belonging to those who had fled. It was not in their interest to see them return. Conversely in Uganda, the refugees included most of those who had ruled the country for decades, without sharing power and without any scruples. For them, negotiating their return inevitably meant losing a significant share of the power which they claimed in its entirety, Therefore the only way to return was by force.

The hardliners won on all fronts: the refugee question was not solved. As a consequence, the few thousand refugees in 1962, who could easily have been integrated into society, grew to 600,000 in 1994.As you know, they did not return to Rwanda through negotiations but by force. Meanwhile a genocide had taken place.

As a priest I wonder about the conditions in which Rwandans were converted to Christianity. The conversion of the king led to the conversion of his subjects. Did it lead to the conversion of their souls? I am baffled by the faith of some Rwandans who were converted. Is it necessary to recall that adherence to Christianity meant exemption from certain duties? There is a fairly substantial difference between the social practices of the rituals of the Church - let's say piety or devotion - and intimate adherence to the evangelical message expressed through the practice of faith. During the genocide I saw people wearing a medal of the Virgin Mary around their neck and holding a machete. We are forced to ask ourselves questions.

André Sibomana
in 'Hope For Rwanda'

God, we are sorry

God, we are sorry:
sorry that we ignore you,
thinking of our own needs and desires and ignoring yours;
wanting to show how good we are
when, in fact, we are not good at all;
parading our skills and virtues
when we should be acknowledging their source.

Give us a humble heart
And listening ears to hear your word to us:
**'Share bread with all the hungry,
give shelter to the poor,
and cover up the naked
then I will be your guide.'**

God, we are sorry:
sorry that we demean others,
dwelling on our own values while ignoring theirs;
hurting instead of consoling,
belittling instead of affirming,
rejecting instead of accepting,
despising instead of loving.

Give us a humble heart
And listening ears to hear your word to us:
**'Share bread with all the hungry,
give shelter to the poor,
and cover up the naked
then I will be your guide.'**

(The response can be sung to Laudate Omnes Gentes,
Rejoice & Sing 403)

Blessing

The largest Protestant church body in the Netherlands has approved the blessing of same-sex partnerships, at a joint meeting of the three synods of the Uniting Protestant Churches in the Netherlands (UPCN). Couples who seek a church blessing must show that their relationship is a lasting one based on love and fidelity, according to by-laws approved by the synods that will go into effect when the three churches that constitute the UPCN finally merge. The UPCN, representing 2.7 million Christians, includes the CWM member church, the Netherlands Reformed Church.

Co-operation

Amsterdam's Free University, which serves theologians of the Uniting Protestant Churches in the Netherlands as well as other churches, has appointed the country's first professor of Pentecostal studies, and thus moved closer to the Pentecostal churches. Professor Cees van der Laan took up his post as Professor of Pentecostal theology and history last autumn while continuing as director of the Azusa Theological Seminary which serves the United Pentecostal and Gospel congregations. In promoting ' the interdisciplinary study of Pentecostalism and Charismatic renewal', the post fits the policy of the theology faculty of the Free University. The relocation of the Azusa seminary from Lunteren to Amsterdam, while maintaining its independence, was agreed in 2001.

Pray with the Reformed Churches in the Netherlands (CWM Europe region).

Rainbow God
you set a colourful bow in the sky and made a promise to all creation:
no matter how sinful humanity may be, your grace still shines.

In the red we see blood:
the blood of millions slaughtered in our selfishness.
Help us to be thankful for the blood of Christ spilled for us.

In the orange we see a fruit:
food to feed the millions of people starving in our world.
Help us to trade more fairly that all may be satisfied.

Yellow reminds us of spring:
new life, warmth and hope.
Help us to play our part in creating a world of hope for everyone.

Green is so often portrayed as envy:
envy that destroys our trust, setting neighbour against neighbour.
Help us to value each other's gifts and our own.

In the blue we feel the cold of barren lands
where human greed has ravaged creation.
Help us to conserve and preserve your creation.

Indigo is dark,
reminding us of the darker side of all human nature.
Help us to conquer our own darker side through faith in you.

Violet is a frail flower,
showing the frailty of our human lives.
Help us to trust in you, that we may grow in strength.

Rainbow God, shine on us.

Calming curry

When racial tension exploded into street riots in Oldham in Lancashire over a scorching holiday weekend in 2001, the Home Office sent an official to review the causes. Faith leaders in the English town were invited to voice their opinions, and over curry in a local restaurant they exchanged views and found new friendships. One consequence, on the following Christmas Day, was a phone call from Imam Shafiq-ur-Rahman to Congregational minister Neil Chappel to give Christmas greetings to his family and the members of Greenacres Church in the Congregational Federation.

The following month, at the urging of the UK Islamic Mission, Imam Rahman suggested holding an Eid celebration at the church, to which Greencares enthusiastically responded, sending out invitations to local churches and mosques and leaders of the local community. On Sunday February 24, 120 people gathered to hear greetings from Churches Together in Oldham and Oldham Council, a reading from the Quran explaining the Eid festival and a stirring address from Professor Ahmed, an Islamic scholar from Wolverhampton University, on moral values in a secular society. Everyone then sat down in the church hall to a curry supper which had been brought by members of the mosque. An Inter-Faith Committee has now been established in Oldham, linking communities which in the past had mixed very infrequently.

Pray with churches of the Congregational Federation (CWM European Region).

*At one hundred years old Abram became Abraham, the father of a son
and father of all nations, because God made a covenant:
a covenant with Abraham, his son and all generations.*

Strengthening God,
as you promised new life to Abraham and Sarah
so you promise new life for us.

When we are suffering:
in mental or physical pain,
**revive our broken spirits,
rekindle our faith
and remind us of your promise.**

When we are persecuted:
suffering injustice, hatred, war;
abandoned or rejected by human friends,
**renew our sense of worth,
rekindle our faith
and remind us of your promise.**

When we think that all is well,
life is good and we are at peace,
**reaffirm our faith,
give us thankful hearts
and remind us of your promise
given not because we deserve it
but through your grace.**

Dementia care

The social service arm of the Presbyterian Church of Aotearoa New Zealand has expanded its mental health care facilities in the city of Nelson. Presbyterian Support, which has been offering daycare and activities for older people with Alzheimer's disease and related dementias in the Nelson district, has recently opened a community house for the long-term mentally ill in Nelson. 'For a long time there has been a group of people with mental ill health who have not been well catered for,' said Presbyterian Support's executive director John Elvidge. 'A 45-year-old man with long term mental health issues might be living in an aged care rest home surrounded by people 40 years older than himself simply because there is nowhere else for him to live.'

Pray with the Presbyterian Church of Aotearoa New Zealand (CWM Pacific region).

God, you spoke:

'You shall have no other gods before me.'
Turn us from the worship of gods of wealth, power and happiness.
'You shall not make for yourself an idol.'
When we worship buildings or traditions make us think again.
'You shall not make wrongful use of the name of the Lord your God.'
If we swear, aloud or silently, open our ears to what we are saying.
'Remember the sabbath day and keep it holy.'
There are so many competing Sunday activities. Help us to put you first.
'Honour your father and mother.'
Respect for our parents is disappearing. Help us to lead by example.
'You shall not murder.'
Give us voice to decry the atrocities of individuals and governments.
'You shall not commit adultery.'
Heal and strengthen those whose relationships are broken by infidelity.
'You shall not steal.'
Credit card fraud, shoplifting – help both victims and perpetrators of theft.
'You shall not bear false witness against your neighbour.'
Help us to get to know our neighbour, and to love each other
'You shall not covet…anything that belongs to your neighbour.'
We live in an age of consumerism. Speak to us about your values.

God, you spoke
and the people did not hear.
You speak today
and still we do not hear.
Give us listening ears and a humble heart
to hear and receive your word.

30 March
Mothering Sunday

Numbers 21:4-9
Psalm 107:1-3, 17-22
Ephesians 2:1-10
John 3:14-21

A mother's story

From Zambia:
I saw two boys and a girl between 6 and 13 years old picking up kernels of maize. I asked them to show me where their mother was. We found her at home lying on a reed mat. When I asked her what she did for a living she looked at me for some time, then looked down and sighed.

'My husband was discharged from the army in 1994,' she began. 'He was our sole breadwinner. I was a fulltime housewife and mother. Food was never a problem, and everything was well with us. Things changed after my husband left the army. He did not receive his benefits for two years, which meant the family had no income. My husband could not cope and died of depression in 1997. Though his benefits came before he died, most of the money went to repay the debts we had accumulated. We often went without a good meal for several days. I tried to sell vegetables, but everyone else sold vegetables too.

'I had no choice but to send the children to beg in town and glean the maize that dropped from trucks passing along the road. But this was no solution... Against my own will, against my faith, I became a walker. I slept with men for money. At first it tormented me and I found it extremely hard to understand. Today I do it with less difficulty.

'Don't ask me about sexually transmitted diseases. I may or may not be a carrier. But as long as I can afford a meal for my family I am happy. I know that one day sooner or later I will die of AIDS. But I can tell you that I find hunger more deadly than AIDS. AIDS kills in years, but hunger kills in days.'

*J K Sampa
in Zambian Church Quarterly*

Unjustified complaints

Read **Numbers 21:4-9**

The Israelites moaned and complained:
Why have you brought us out of Egypt
only to die in the wilderness?

Still today we moan and complain:

'I'm hungry. What's for dinner?'
But around me the starving
have nothing for breakfast, lunch or dinner
except scraps scavenged on the streets and rubbish tips.
How shall we feed them?

'I don't have enough money.'
But in every town and city the poor
have no money at all,
begging and relying on charity.
How should we give?

'My friend isn't speaking to me.'
But even today there are those
who are persecuted for their beliefs,
victims of war and prejudice,
refugees fleeing their own land.
Can we speak out for them?

God of the Israelites,
be our God.
As we travel through this time of Lent
open our eyes and hearts to the love of the cross.
Bring us out of the darkness of our own self-pity
and into the light of life in Christ
so that we can share his generosity with others.

Bishop moves out

The Roman Catholic Bishop of Lancaster in England announced last year that he was selling his £1 m official home, using much of the proceeds on relieving the problems of the poor and becoming 'a bishop on the move'. Describing Bishop's House in Lancaster as a beautiful 16-room Victorian mansion, Bishop Patrick O'Donoghue said that he wanted to demonstrate to his people, and to others, that the Church is more than big houses which are status symbols from another era.

'We need to look at our structures,' he said, 'otherwise we are going to end up as caretakers of mausoleums rather than as care-takers of the poor. My job is not that of managing director of The Church plc, but servant of the word of God and shepherd of the flock.'

Most of the money raised from the sale will go to projects aimed at easing deprivation and drug problems. Some of it will go to inter-faith projects.

When Jesus, in his days as man,
addressed you, God, in prayer,
his tears revealed his suffering,
his cries - despair.

Although he was your son on earth
we nailed him to a cross.
But now in heaven he pleads for us:
our pain and loss.

You offer hope, eternal life,
if we can glimpse the light
and think of others, not ourselves,
affirming right.

We try to live obediently
to see your work is done.
Lord, send your love and grant us peace,
through Christ, your son.

This can be sung to Wicklow or St Cuthbert *(Rejoice & Sing 330)*

Liturgy of the Palms Psalm 118:1-2, 19-29; John 12:12-16
Liturgy of the Passion Isaiah 50:4-9a; Psalm 31:9-16;
Philippians 2:5-11; Mark 14:1-15, or Mark 15:1-39

Palm Sunday and Passion Sunday

Read   Psalm 118:1-2, 19-29; John 12:12-16

The crowds in the city came out to meet you
with great, if misplaced, expectation.
The people who had been with you all the time
didn't understand.

Prophecy can be fulfilled,
but often in ways we don't expect.

Hammer at the gates of our hearts, Lord,
demanding to be let in.
Let us welcome your humble entrance, and welcome the donkey,
for your sake.
Give us a sure foundation
and bind our broken archways into your kingdom.

We would follow you into your city
and enter into your triumph.

For you are blessed.
You save us.
You are our God.
And we give thanks to you;
we celebrate you and sing your praise.

Hosanna in the highest!

**O give thanks to the Lord, for he is good
His steadfast love endures for ever.**

Always among you

John 12:8   The poor you have always among you, but you will not always have me.

We may feel like challenging both of these statements of Jesus (which do not appear in all the manuscripts of John's Gospel and may have been inserted from Matthew 26). Many of us, while acknowledging that there are today far more poor people than there were in Jesus' time, dislike the note of inevitability in the first statement, which echoes Deuteronomy 15.11: 'There will never cease to be some in need on the earth'. We don't like to sit down under such a statement, we want to alter it, with our concern for marginalised people in our own communities, our Christian Aid giving, our Fair Trade and Drop the Debt lobbying, and maybe with our vote. If we accept that there will always be some in need, aren't we giving up the struggle, diluting our hopes for the coming of the kingdom of God? It was true in the first century in the home of Lazarus, but is it really a word for today?

And 'you will not always have me' was physically true of the man Jesus in that Passover week, but what does it say to a 21st century Christian believer? We want to assert that we still have Jesus; he is always with us. Is this whole verse really for us in 2003?

Maybe we should change our sights, put on Gospel spectacles. A world in which no-one is in need is a frozen world, a world with no place for struggle, or service or sacrifice. Perhaps we can imagine it to be true today in one west end city street, in some holiday brochure village, but behind their glossy images there is poverty and need and an opportunity for loving service. And Jesus is not always heard there. Look around you, and listen.

Read   Isaiah 42:1-9; John 12:1-14

Lord, I thank you from the bottom of my heart
that you don't shout at me
like so many who proclaim their certainties,
that you come to me in the quiet,
that you support my bruised personality
and don't put out my flickering faith.

You created the heavens and stretched them out:
recreate me and stretch my capacities.
You spread out the earth and give breath to those who walk in it:
spread out your love over me, and sustain my life.

Martha had gone through much –
a dead brother, the absence of the one who might have saved him.
Yet her hope was fulfilled, her faith restored.
When my faith and my hope are bruised and burning dimly,
help me to pour out to you the things I treasure,
in trust that you will pass through death with me
and in gratitude for new life.

So many questions

John 12:21   Some Gentiles approached Philip: 'Sir, we would like to see Jesus'.

12:29   A voice came from heaven... the crowd said it was thunder they heard.

12:34   'What do you mean... What Son of Man is this?'

12:36   Jesus went away from them into hiding.

The last verses in this chapter are sometimes entitled 'The end of public discourse' - the end of Jesus' public ministry, to the world and to the Jews at large - and still many found him a mystery. The Gentiles visiting Jerusalem at the Passover festival want to see this Jesus. The stories about him are intriguing; they have questions to ask, which seeing him may help to satisfy. John, the Gospel-writer, hears God speaking in affirmation of Jesus' life and message, but the crowd hear only thunder.

Even the well-versed Temple pilgrims are baffled by the idea that Jesus is not arriving but departing. 'Our law teaches us that the Messiah remains for ever.' But this possible Messiah talks of leaving; and even before the darkness he is foretelling, he slips away into hiding.

John has two comments on all this bafflement, these unanswered questions. In spite of the many signs Jesus had performed, they would not believe him, their eyes were shut; and even those who believed would not acknowledge him, for fear of being banned from the synagogue We have our questions and our hesitations too, perhaps about Jesus' full humanity and his divinity. At this moment in Holy Week he seems to be a person living in two worlds, drawing nearer and nearer to the interface. Ponder John's answers.

Tuesday of Holy Week

Lord, we have often entered upon tasks for you
which at the time seemed huge
and yet we have found that they were greater than we thought;
for you always have bigger things for us to do
than those we think are within our capacity.

Which is the more foolish –
us for the miscalculations of our strength,
or you for entrusting us with great things?

Those Greeks in John's Gospel (we don't hear any more about them),
Were they just curious, or trusting?
We all have to start somewhere.
The corn is so small,
so apparently inert,
yet you enable it to be productive.

Make us ready to face the death
which brings us fulfilment and life.
Make us come to you, like those Greeks.
To your glory, Lord.

Devil's man

John 13:27 Satan entered into him.

One Bible scholar suggests that in chapter 12 John describes Judas as a thief, possessed by avarice, to explain his treachery. Our minds are stuffed with other possible reasons for Judas' kiss: he was a Zealot for whom Jesus did not move fast or decisively enough against Rome; he thought that a confrontation between Jesus and the authorities would spark off the freedom movement. John's explanation is that the devil took possession of him.

More specifically, John says that the devil entered Judas as he took the bread which Jesus had broken. The moment of blessing became the moment of betrayal. A companion whom Jesus had chosen, called and taught, who had shared the journeys and the hardships of his teacher, could still turn against him. For centuries some have said that Judas' betrayal was simply a part of God's plan, a fearful but necessary act in the drama of our salvation. His part was written for him. Today we may be inclined to see Judas' action as a sign of the fault-line in our humanity, evidence that dedication to God and daily prayer cannot arm us invincibly against wrongdoing or wrong thinking.

To our generation, perhaps more than ever before, the weaknesses and flaws of the great and good, the heroes of the Christian faith even, are constantly being exposed. We need the strengthening fellowship of the followers of Jesus, and they need ours.

Read   Isaiah 50:4-9a; Hebrews 12:1-3; John 13:21-32

Lord, you could face the spitting,
the pulling out of hairs,
the insults and the blows
because you had persevered in the truth.

But the betrayal of a friend
troubled your spirit.
'Do it quickly,' you said
lest the flint of your face should crack
with the breaking of your heart.

It was to the glory of God,
you said.
It was more than we want to go through
for the glory of your name.
Help us to persevere
as we face hardship, mockery, perhaps even torture.
Because you went there first
you can make our faith, our faltering faith,
perfect
and cause us not to lose heart
as we see the glory of the Father
revealed in you.

A Call to Communion

At this table Jesus calls us to sit and eat with him.
We who accept this invitation are those he loves, who want to love him in return;
who are hungry and thirsty for the bread of life which he offers and the wine which he pours out for us in love and self-sacrifice;
who have sought to be in love and charity with our neighbours,
who have asked God's pardon for our sins, and are glad to accept his cleansing and his strength with which to live;
who have seen God's kingdom of righteousness being established in the world and who long to eat and drink in that kingdom;
who are eager to share in Christ's work in the world.
So sit, and eat, and drink. He gave his life for you, and here he shares it with you. Rejoice that you are called to the Lord's supper with his friends.

Unless I wash you

Read   Exodus 12:1-14; John 13:1-17, 31b-35

The lamb had no choice in the matter
if your word was to be fulfilled.
But each year salvation was remembered with joy
through the slaughter of the lamb.

Jesus had no choice in the matter:
he, too, was slaughtered,
and we remember him in a feast
which also recalls our salvation.

But feasts are not enough.
Help us, Lord, in humility to serve each other,
to wash and be washed –
all the dirty bits which, perhaps, we would rather
that others do not see.

**Now is the Son of Man glorified
And God is glorified in him.**

Keep us, Lord, as your disciples,
in loving communion and service,
one with another
and all with you.

For all the world to hear

John 18:20   Jesus replied...

In Mark's Gospel and in Matthew's, Jesus is noticeably silent under questioning. In Luke, Herod, who was 'longing to question him', gets no replies. In John's Gospel, however, Jesus is eloquent and forceful. Before the High Priest:: 'I have spoken openly for all the world to hear... I have said nothing in secret.' Before Pilate: '"King" is your word. My task is to bear witness to the truth.'

We are often more mindful of Isaiah's prophecy: As a sheep before her shearers is dumb, so he opened not his mouth. But John's Jesus is not a mute sufferer. He speaks openly of God to Jewish leader and Roman governor. Here, perhaps, is the confrontation Judas was hoping for, though Judas could not have understood how Jesus was, in fact, the victor. Like his life, his trial bears witness to God's truth.

It was Peter, following Jesus to the High Priest's house, faithful and yet fearful, who avoided the questions. By the shared warmth of the courtyard fire he could not confront the cold mockery (would it have been anything worse?) of being seen as one of Them and not part of the uncommitted crowd of onlookers. William Temple explains that the maid on duty at the door asked Peter a question framed to expect the answer no. And Peter 'slid into the place prepared for him'. *I am not.*

There are times when we are offered the easy way out of the hard question. It is not always about acknowledging Jesus, but it is often about denying the truth.

The cup the Father has given me

Read   Isaiah 52:13-53:12; John 18:1-19, 42

Lord, you were lifted up, as Isaiah wrote,
your face scarred, your hands and feet pierced,
victim of injustice, political scheming and religious hatred;
despised, rejected, ignored, pain-wracked, blood-stained.

He bore the sin of many and made intercession for us.

The king of the Jews
They said you made this claim: they said you were wrong,
but Pilate stood his ground.
You are the King of the Jews, ruling from the Cross,
and our King, ruling our lives.

He bore the sin of many and made intercession for us.

Woman, here is your son … here is your mother
Broken families, broken lives,
battered women, neglected children …
Healer of divisions, healer of wounds,
from your cross you bring new hope and new relationships of love.

He bore the sin of many and made intercession for us.

I am thirsty … It is finished
The cup is almost drained, and still he thirsts,
but through his blood it is filled again;
his work is accomplished.

He bore the sins of many and made intercession for us.

Job 14:1-14
Psalm 31:1-4, 15-16
1 Peter 4:1-8
John 19:38-42

Garden tomb

John 19:41   a new tomb, not yet used for burial

In South Africa - and in other countries? - you may see, propped against the wall of a secondhand shop, a used coffin for sale. We who bury coffins to rot, or burn them, find this bizarre and unnerving, but parts of the world where every resource may be recycled have fewer qualms. John emphasises that Jesus' body was laid in a new tomb, an unused tomb befitting the burial of the Lord of life. John alone of the Gospellers places the tomb in a garden.

For generations Christian pilgrims to Jerusalem have been shown the garden tomb, outside the city walls but far from Golgotha, which was suggested by General Gordon as a possible site for Jesus' burial. The significance of a garden, in John's thinking, is not our vision of a green place of peace and new life, but possibly to link Jesus' death with two other gardens: the garden of Eden where men and women lost their companionship with God; and the garden of Gethsemane, where Jesus was finally betrayed to his enemies. The garden tomb, which could not hold his body, reverses our defeats in those other gardens.

Read   Job 14:1-14; John 19:38-42

A blank day.
Behind that blank wall of stone lies hope, dead.
The blankness of dead hope and the numbness of bereavement
make us devoid of feeling.
Mortals die and are laid low:
humans expire, and where are they?
If mortals die, will they live again?

Like Job, we find the future blank,
the Immortal not deaf but dead.

The spices will not console;
they only mask the stench of death.
Where is he now?
We had hoped …
but hope is dead.

Awaiting the Day of Preparation:
for what do we prepare?
Death lays its hand upon our souls;
our minds and hearts are numb.

But behind the scenes, behind the stone,
who knows what is going on?
Is there preparation for release?
We would hope … but hope is dead.

Unless …
then we could wait for release from service,
for release from the tomb.
Preparation would be worthwhile.
So, on this blank day
we wait for the stirring of dead hope,
and pray.

Acts 10:34-43
Psalm 118:1-2, 14-24
1 Corinthians 15:1-11
John 20:1-18

From star to cross

The journey was not long from Bethlehem to Calvary,
from star to cross;
what loss.

Thirty years of preparation,
three short years of love;
what cost.

On this day the price was paid
for love that went astray.
On this day our Lord was raised
for all the world to say,
God is good, let earth adore
the Prince who came
not as a king but poor,
and with his life gave life to all,
just once
upon a cross;
what loss;
what cost;
what love.
The love that burns within our hearts
when through a veil of tears we
hear our name and recognise
the voice that calls as
Jesus.
Can we be quiet?
Can we hide our joy,
would we not celebrate
with words beyond this world
the all-encompassing witness to the wonder…
                    for God so loved the world.

Read   **Psalm 118; Acts 10:34-43**

Give thanks to the Lord for he is good.

The Lord is our strength and our power.
He has become our salvation.
We shall not die but we shall live
for he did not give us over to death.

Here and now you have broken into our lives.
You have become the cornerstone of our faith.
With you there is hope
for you did not give in to death;
you conquered death.
The stone was rolled away
and you were not entombed
within the darkness of death.
Instead the light of life shines
within and around you.
You are alive
and through you we live.

Here and now we celebrate with awe and wonder,
God's love for us.
We hear the news;
and feel the buzz;
we rush to share the news,
for we have seen the Lord.
He is here
and he is calling to the world,
come and follow me.

Let us share the light of love,
for we have seen the Lord.

The Bridge

In the beginning was God.
Then God created the world
but the world loved itself
and not God;
so God sent his Son to rescue the world,
and even the darkness of the world
could not quench the light of the Son,
though it tried.
The Son became the Saviour of the world
and the light grows stronger
with each heart that is opened.
The Son became the bridge
between despair and hope
and invites all to cross the bridge
while the darkness sits beneath
threatening and waiting.
Some cannot yet see the bridge,
their journey has not yet found it;
some sense its presence,
glimpse it from a distance,
but cannot find the way.
One day they will see it
And, emboldened by love,
they will step upon the bridge
and feel the power surge through them;
power to release them from guilt and shame;
power to enable them to new and amazing wonders;
power that comes only from God.
And beneath, the darkness still waits
but its threat is gone.

Praying with
CWM churches

2003

Council for World Mission
a global community of churches

AFRICA

Church of Jesus Christ in Madagascar (FJKM)

Madagascar has been troubled by political unrest over the past few years. The FJKM has been at the centre of work towards a peaceful resolution.

Give thanks:
- For the success of the lay trainers' scheme in Madagascar.

Pray:
- For political stability in the country;
- For the renewal of mission work through the training of ministers and evangelists;
- For the church's village health centres, orphanages, schools, village co-operatives, and handicraft centres;
- For spiritual renewal in the church.

A church service in the capital, Antananarivo. The CWM member Church of Jesus Christ in Madagascar is among the largest denominations in the country.

Churches of Christ in Malawi (CCM)

Give thanks:

* For the youth committee's work in spreading the good news and helping the needy.

Pray:

* For those affected by famine in Malawi;
* For increased co-operation of the church's finance, projects and mission programmes so it can be more effective in its mission;
* That youth and women's activities in the church will continue to flourish;
* That God will give strength and good health to retired ministers.

United Church of Zambia (UCZ)

The UCZ is continuing to grow at a fast rate, putting a strain on its resources, including its pastors.

Give thanks:

* For the recent growth of the UCZ.

Pray:

* For peace and stability in Africa;
* For the church's efforts to tackle HIV/AIDS;
* For full women's participation in all areas of church life;
* For the evangelistic initiatives to areas in Zambia that have not heard the Word of God.

© NICK SIREAU/CWM

Young men work on a project for people with special needs run by the United Church of Zambia.

United Congregational Church of Southern Africa (UCCSA)

The UCCSA is a transnational church, spanning Botswana, Mozambique, Namibia, South Africa and Zimbabwe.

Give thanks:
- For the appointment of a new general secretary, Steve Titus, and the new treasurer, Robin Thompson;
- For the UCCSA's partnership with CWM;
- For the relative calm and stability throughout the countries in which the UCCSA operates.

Pray:
- For a smooth beginning for the South African Synod;
- For peace and justice to prevail in Zimbabwe where violence continues to trouble people's lives.

Uniting Presbyterian Church in Southern Africa (UPCSA)

The UPCSA comprises presbyteries in South Africa, Zambia and Zimbabwe.

Give thanks:
- For the courageous witness of the ministers and members in Zimbabwe during the political upheaval;
- For continued growth in church membership in Zambia.

© NICK SIREAU/CWM

Pray:
- For church members from different nations and cultures to grow in unity and understanding;
- For all congregations to support financially the work of the UPCSA;
- For the development of a mission statement and mission priorities to give the UPCSA direction;
- For the government of Zimbabwe and the role of the church in particular in speaking out for justice.

A woman stands outside her shack in a South African shanty town where members of the Uniting Presbyterian Church run an outreach project.

CARIBBEAN

Guyana Congregational Union (GCU)

Pray:

- For the GCU's outreach to indigenous peoples;
- For congregations to be effective witnesses in their local area;
- That the GCU's leaders will be filled with wisdom;
- That the church responds to new religious movements.

United Church in Jamaica and the Cayman Islands (UCJCI)

As Jamaican society feels the impact of poverty, violence and drug abuse, the UCJCI is developing new initiatives to strengthen communities.

Give thanks:

- For the work of the Institute for Theological and Leadership Development in building leaders for the future.

Pray:

- For an end to politically-motivated violence in Jamaica, especially during elections;
- That men will learn to take more responsibility for their families;
- For the church's outreach to prostitutes and drug addicts.

© NICK SIREAU/CWM

Sunday worship with the United Church, Grand Cayman. Christianity runs deep in Caribbean culture and churches are often full.

EAST ASIA

Gereja Presbyterian Malaysia (GPM)

The GPM is furthering its mission sensitively in Malaysia's multifaith society. It is increasingly combining social action with evangelism.

Pray:
- For the success of missions to unreached people in east Malaysia;
- That the church's social action projects will demonstrate Christ's love to the needy;
- For the GPM's response to growing social ills like drug abuse;
- For the reputation of the church in a Muslim-dominated country.

© NICK SIREAU/CWM

Lively worship at a Presbyterian congregation in Johor Bahru, Malaysia. The Malaysian church is vibrant and outgoing.

Hong Kong Council of the Church of Christ in China (HKCCCC)

Pray:
- For the HKCCCC's youth leadership training programme;
- For sharing of experience and resources with the mainland Chinese church;
- For the people of Hong Kong facing high unemployment and economic recession;
- For the second term of the chief executive of the Hong Kong Special Administrative Region government.

Presbyterian Church in Singapore (PCS)

Give thanks:

- For God's amazing provisions during the PCS's 120th anniversary celebrations;
- For a strong sense of unity between the PCS's English-speaking and Chinese-speaking congregations.

Pray:

- That God will provide the resources for full-time personnel in communications and church networking;
- For more church members to respond to the call of full-time pastoral service;
- That God will provide the effective leadership needed for the church to meet the challenges ahead;
- For the Presbyterian Community Services as they build up childcare work and a school for children with special educational needs;
- That the English and Chinese presbyteries will pool their resources effectively in overseas missionary work.

© Nick Sireau/CWM

A traditional service at Orchard Road Presbyterian church, Singapore. The church has several services on Sundays to cater to different languages and nationalities.

Presbyterian Church in Taiwan (PCT)

The PCT is at the forefront of campaigning for democracy and social justice in Taiwan. It particularly focuses on the rights of marginalised tribal people.

Give thanks:
• That democracy is developing in Taiwan.

Pray:
• For security in relations with China;
• For the PCT's church-planting initiatives;
• For the protection of Taiwan's environment, particularly in the vulnerable tribal areas;
• That the church's Seamen's and Fishermen's Centre will continue to uphold the rights of those who work at sea.

Aboriginal children in Taiwan's highlands. Many tribal people live in poor conditions.

Presbyterian Church of Korea (PCK)

Pray:
• For the efforts to reunite North and South Korea;
• For closer co-operation between denominations in Korea;
• For the church's acceptance of disabled people.

EUROPE

Congregational Federation (CF)

Give thanks:

- For the appointment of Stephen Haward as national children's and youth worker;
- For mission partners from the wider CWM family serving the CF in the UK;
- For the increasing contribution of women at all levels within the CF.

Pray:

- For local congregations considering afresh their ministry and mission;
- For the CF's Integrated Training Course for ministers and laity and its ongoing development;
- For the children and youth of the churches.

Rev Janet Wootton leads a Congregational church that runs a successful project for the homeless.

Presbyterian Church of Wales (PCW)

The PCW grew out of the 18th century Methodist revival and has a strong missionary thrust. In recent years it has found it difficult to adapt its mission strategy to a rapidly changing and secularised society.

The church has a range of mission projects and (with partner churches) has strong links with the National Assembly for Wales, established in 1999.

Give thanks:

- For Coleg Trefeca, the historic centre of the denomination and now its lay training centre;
- For the growth in ecumenical partnerships in Wales;
- For the first term of the National Assembly for Wales and for its achievements in providing co-ordinated democratic government for the nation.

Pray:
- That the new general secretary, Rev Ifan Roberts, and other newly appointed staff, work together as an effective leadership team;
- For pastorates seeking ministers or lay mission partners;
- For growth in understanding between the Welsh and English language churches and between those of different cultures and backgrounds in Wales;
- For the new arrangements for training the ministerial candidates in the University of Wales;
- That those elected to the National Assembly for Wales and to local authorities in Wales in 2003 may be committed to serving the people.

Reformed Churches in the Netherlands (RCN)

The Reformed Churches in the Netherlands is uniting with the Netherlands Reformed Church and the Evangelical Lutheran Church in the Kingdom of the Netherlands. These are among the largest Reformed denominations, with a declining membership in a secularising and multicultural society.

Give thanks:
- For those congregations that are growing;
- For the faithfulness of many volunteers who form the backbone of the local congregations;
- For the success of the young people's voluntary year of service;
- For deepening relations and understanding with migrant churches in the Netherlands.

Pray:
- For the successful completion of the process of unification;
- That the churches find ways to communicate the gospel in a secularised society;
- That the churches will speak clearly for justice and mercy in the debate on asylum and immigration;
- For the church to participate effectively in discussions and campaigns on globalisation, the international financial system and climate change.

Union of Welsh Independents (UWI)

The UWI has around 500 churches conducting its ministry through the Welsh language in England and Wales.

Like so many of its sister churches throughout the Europe region, it finds it difficult to reach people. A great deal of effort is being made to find ways of promoting its work among children and young people, but the energy and commitment required is often lacking.

Give thanks:
- For those churches that have been guided by the publication of the booklet, Our Crisis, Our Opportunity, to find new ways of being church;
- For the continual generosity of so many congregations that support the missionary work and spread the good news of Christ.

Pray:
- That the church will respond effectively and confidently to moral, social and spiritual decline in the community;
- That the church will give due attention to the needs of the family by encouraging its members to devote time for daily meditation and prayer;
- That the churches be challenged by the Holy Spirit to seek a clear path through the destructive effects of secularism.

United Reformed Church (URC)
The URC exists in England, Scotland and Wales. In recent years it has become more aware of its multicultural context, seeking to include the Afro-Caribbean, Ghanaian, Korean and Pakistani communities (among others) in its life. Its witness is to a secular society.

Give thanks:
- For the church's unity in Christ;
- That children and young people continue to play an important part in the life of the church;
- For new mission projects in many local churches and communities;
- For congregations' increasing support of partner organisations overseas.

Pray:
- For the new general secretariat team, David Cornick and Ray Adams;
- For those who look after the church's finances at a time of difficulty;
- For ecumenical conversations with sister churches, locally and nationally;
- For the witness of small congregations where mission needs and opportunities are immense.

PACIFIC

Congregational Christian Church in American Samoa (CCCAS)

Pray:
- For the younger generation which needs God's help to face consumerism and drug abuse in a fast-changing world;
- That the churches will be equipped with God's Word as they spread the gospel;
- For the church as it deals with new religious movements;
- For the church's work to strengthen the family in American Samoa;
- For the church's response to rising social problems such as drug and alcohol abuse.

Women from the village of Laulii, American Samoa.

Congregational Christian Church in Samoa (CCCS)

The CCCS is a transnational church with members in seven countries, including New Zealand and Australia. Nearly half of Samoa's population is associated with the Congregational Church.

Give thanks:
- For the church's successful youth programmes.

Pray:
- For the church training programmes, pastors' schools and youth leaders;
- For the development of church schools;
- For the church as it faces rising sea levels due to global warming;
- That the church will find a way to respond to the high youth suicide rate.

Congregational Union of New Zealand (CUNZ)

Pray:

- That young people will continue to develop their commitment to the church;
- For new leaders to take the church forward;
- For closer relations with the Protestant church in the island nation of Niue;
- For the church's efforts to promote gender equality.

Ekalesia Kelisiano Tuvalu (EKT)

Pray:

- For action to combat the increasing threat of rising sea levels;
- For a solution to the problems surrounding the settlement of asylum-seekers in the Pacific region;
- For the nation's leaders to rule with wisdom and integrity.

Kiribati Protestant Church (KPC)

Kiribati is made up of tiny islands spanning hundreds of kilometres, making communication difficult. Despite this, the church is increasing its mission thrust.

Give thanks:

- For effective outreach to communities through island councils, congregations, youth and women's groups.

Pray:

- For more qualified teachers for the church schools;
- For the church's mission to inactive and backsliding church members;
- For the Training of Trainers programme to prepare pastors, evangelists and congregations to reach beyond congregational boundaries;
- For the success of the church's self-support projects that seek to provide much needed income.

Nauru Congregational Church (NCC)

Pray:

- For the arts and craft centre which will include a classroom devoted to leadership training;
- For new means of economic survival now that the island's main source of revenue, its phosphate reserves, are depleted;
- For the church to resist the influence of newly-arrived sects in Nauru.

Presbyterian Church of Aotearoa New Zealand (PCANZ)

Pray:

- For the new initiatives in working with children and young families;
- For the church's support of the indigenous Maori community;
- That each parish in the church take on the challenges of lay leadership;
- For all staff and ministers who work to share the gospel.

St John's Presbyterian church, Auckland. The church building also hosts a Korean Presbyterian church and a Pacific Islanders' fellowship.

United Church in Papua New Guinea (UCPNG)

Pray:

- That the church responds well to changes in society;
- For the success of projects to prevent the spread of HIV/AIDS;
- For peace in Bougainville and healing of ethnic divisions.

United Church in Solomon Islands (UCSI)

Ethnic conflict is tearing the Solomon Islands apart. The UCSI is playing a vital role in sustaining the community.

Give thanks:

- For 100 years of the gospel in the Solomon Islands.

Pray:

- For peace and reconciliation as the country recovers from ethnic conflict;
- That men and women work together as equals in the church and society;
- For the church's engagement in mission and evangelism;
- For the work of the church hospital in caring for the sick.

SOUTH ASIA

Church of Bangladesh (CoB)

The CoB is highly active in social development despite its small size. It provides much needed support to the nation.

Pray:
- For peace between the different religions in Muslim-majority Bangladesh;
- For the church's programmes to protect the environment;
- For the church's programme to raise awareness about naturally-occurring arsenic contamination in the water.

A young girl at a village for abandoned children run by the Church of Bangladesh.

Church of North India (CNI)

Give thanks:
- That people of different faiths can live together peacefully;
- For the new Information and Technology Institute with the CNI's Human Potential Development Programme;
- For the church's united witness in social and health development work.

Pray:
- That congregations will rediscover CNI's identity and unity;
- That the church will embody and exhibit an exemplary Christian lifestyle;

- That the church ensures transparency and accountability at all levels;
- For marginalised communities accessing the CNI's education, social and health care services;
- For the CNI to express solidarity in concrete acts with women, children, the disabled, the elderly, tribals and Dalits (untouchables);
- That the church creates healing communities through interfaith initiatives.

Church of South India (CSI)
Pray:
- For the church's work to empower the marginalised Advisai (tribals) and Dalits (untouchables);
- For peace between Tamils and Sinhalese in Sri Lanka;
- For the educational and evangelistic work with tribal people;
- For wisdom among the church's leaders as they plan its mission.

Presbyterian Church of India (PCI)
The PCI is based mainly in Mizoram, a tribal state in north-east India.

Pray:
- For unity between churches in India;
- That the church develops its medical and social work through health care centres, hospitals, schools and rescue homes for displaced women;
- For spiritual revival within worshipping communities.

Presbyterian Church of Myanmar (PCM)
Pray:
- For theological education of pastors;
- For the leadership training among lay people, women and youth;
- For the church's campaign to spread the gospel.

Front cover: Children leave a Congregational Christian Church service in Sapapalii, Samoa – the village where Rev John Williams, a missionary from the London Missionary Society, arrived in 1830. Photo: © Jocelyn Carlin

Council for World Mission, Ipalo House, 32-34 Great Peter Street, London SW1P 2DB, UK
Tel: +44 (0)20 7222 4214   Fax: +44 (0)20 7233 1747 or +44 (0)20 7222 3510
Email: council@cwmission.org.uk   Website: www.cwmission.org.uk
Charity No 232868 registered in the UK
Printed by Healeys Printers, Ipswich, UK

Read   Psalm 133; Acts 4:32-35; 1 John 1:1-2:2

Lord Jesus, you have crossed the chasm
between God and the world.
and in you we are linked
to God
and to one another.
Gathered here, joined in love,
we rejoice in God's gift,
a gift that ties the cradle to the cross,
and spans all who believe.

How pleasant and good is unity.
Help us to celebrate all that unites us;
to rejoice in fellowship with one another,
to cherish time spent together,
and opportunities to help one another.
Help us to see through your eyes,
and in the power of the Spirit
to link arms with those in need,
connecting with the outcast,
and traversing the divide between rich and poor.

Lord Jesus, you came
not for one but for all;
you came to save the world
from the darkness of hate:
Bridge of love,
in whom we rejoice
and to whom we bring our thanks.

Acts 3:12-19
Psalm 4
1 John 3:1-7
Luke 24:36b-48

Witnesses to the wonder

While they were talking, Jesus came;
intrusive, uninvited, standing there,
telling them not to be afraid.
Never mind afraid, they were terrified.
Everyone knew he was dead.
Someone had whispered, 'Jesus is alive,'
someone had said they had seen him, but
expecting him to be there, never!
Such things did not happen.

'Touch my hands and feet!'
O such doubt!

'Touch me, see I am real!
Have you anything to eat?
Everything written about me is fulfilled.'

Witnesses to the wonder,
one by one they realised!
Now they could see.
Drawn to touch, they had been touched,
and their eyes were open.
Repent and believe, your sins are forgiven.

Read   Luke 24:36b-48; Acts 3:12-19

Living Lord, you come to us
and we turn away,
closing our eyes
to the reality of your presence.

Living Lord, you reach out and touch us
and we shrug you off,
afraid to believe
in the reality of your presence.

Living Lord, you sit with us
and we share a meal
and still we cannot see
the reality of your presence.

Living Lord, we pray to you
and you heal the sick,
and still we do not believe
in the reality of your presence.

Lord of life,
it is we who are dead;
afraid to believe in a risen Lord.
Help us to believe in the reality of your presence.
Impelled by your invitation
may we respond, allowing ourselves
to doubt our disbelief,
drawn ever closer to your wonder,
disciples of deliverance
for a world trapped in a cage of rationality.
Help us to expect you, to plan for your presence
and celebrate your coming,
for you are our living Lord.

11 May
Christian Aid Week

Acts 4:5-12
Psalm 23
1 John 3:16-24
John 10:11-18

Changing the picture

The year 2002 began badly for Malawi. Food shortages - a perennial problem, especially in the area bordering Mozambique - led the government to declare a state of national emergency. Much of the 2001 harvest, which should have lasted until March, was badly damaged by floods. Because few farmers have livestock they traditionally have little or nothing to sell for food in a bad harvest year. Under the leadership of two local organisations, the Christian Services Committee of Malawi and the Christian Council of Mozambique (both Christian Aid partners), the picture is slowly being changed. Women on both sides of the border are being helped to grow cash crops such as groundnuts and paprika and rear goats and guinea-fowl, to provide food and an alternative income. Traditionally excluded from decision-making, women in 21 villages in Malawi and 15 in Mozambique are learning from the Women's Border Area Development Programme how to help their families with better farming techniques and new boreholes for clean water, as well as finding a place with men in the decision-making in their communities.

Malawi has welcomed three special service groups sent in recent years from Ta'an Presbyterian Church in Taipei City, Taiwan, to help in developing health and education work in the African country. Teams of Taiwanese doctors and nurses have brought medicines and shared their skills, and the teams have noted the need for more religious education and professional training in Malawi.

Pray with Churches of Christ in Malawi (CWM Africa region).

Pray for Christian Aid and the bridge of loving support it provides with people around the world. Pray for its leaders, its staff, its partner organisations, for those who collect for it and for those who give.

Read   1 John 3:16-24

Living God, present in young and old,
inspire us by your Spirit
to love with the simplicity
and trust of children;
leaving aside our grown-up words and speeches;
emptying ourselves of preconceptions.

Challenged by your love,
humbled by your service,
in which least became the greatest,
we lift to you the child within us;
dependent upon you;
revelling in you;
enquiring of you;
nourished by you.

Language divides;
encourage in us an active response
that speaks in sign and symbol,
utilising our gifts
to serve our brothers and sisters.

Loving God, help us to value all people,
offering the open friendship of little children.
Vanquish our pride and prejudice
and enable our love.
In the name of Christ our Saviour.

Acts 8:26-40
Psalm 22:25-31
1 John 4:7-21
John 15:1-8

A prayer to end Christian Aid Week

We dare to pray:
Lord, let the world be changed,
for we long to see the end of poverty.
We dare to pray:
Lord, let the rules be changed,
for we long to see trade bring justice
to the poor.

We dare to pray:
Lord, let our lives be changed,
for we long to bring hope where good news is needed.
In the strength of your Spirit
and inspired by your compassion,
we make this promise to work for change,
and wait confidently for the day
when you make all things new.

Perfected love

So much love, reaching to the ends of the earth:
Father love, sowing seeds of truth;
Mother love, giving birth to new hope;

unceasing,
unchanging,
keeping hold of the world
for eternity.

Perfect love
casting out fear,
celebrating diversity.

Abiding love,
working
to transform and renew.

Caught up in your embrace,
God of love,
your ways are revealed to us.

We see others in your light,
we are offered unexpected gifts
and hear unimagined truths.

We are sustained and challenged,
made one with you
and one with each other.

For the gift of your life
received and shared,
we give you thanks.

Social concern

The United Church of Zambia is asking its ministers to deal with the social issues affecting the country and not simply to concentrate on spiritual issues. A leadership school (funded by partner Churches) was organised by the United Church at the diaconal centre at Kabwe last year to train ministers and evangelists in leadership skills. Bishop Patrice Siyemeto has said that the Church wants its leaders to understand and deal with the ever-changing attitudes of people in society. Like most of southern Africa, Zambia is battling the HIV/AIDS pandemic, which is estimated to affect 20 per cent of its adult population.

Pray with the United Church of Zambia (CWM Africa region).

Read   Acts 10:44-48; John 15:9-17

Week by week
we celebrate your new life.
We hear your new commandment
to love one another
as you have loved us.
We want to sing a new song
in harmony with you.

And yet, embracing the new
might mean letting go of the old
and we're not always ready for that.

Forgive us when we close minds and hearts
to new ways of living,
as if we know it all.

Forgive us when we do not greet
new people with open-hearted love
until we are sure
that they will be like us.

Forgive us when we speak
only of the way we think things should be done
and drown out
quieter voices
that do not have our confidence.

God of compassion,
giver of faith that conquers the world,
reach again into our souls;
transform us through your Spirit
that your friends can become our friends
and your love may be seen in our lives.

The Lord is near

Ascended Jesus:
When we hear of you taken up into heaven
  with the disciples gazing wistfully after you;
  seated at the right hand of God;
   gone from us to be with your Father and our Father,
    rearrange the picture-book of our minds.
Show us yourself walking with us in Huddersfield and Harlech;
  seated beside us, around the communion table
   and around the breakfast table;
  in our house as clearly as in the Father's house –
  more clearly, since our picture of the Father's house is
   shakier than the knowledge of our own.
Take the crick out of our necks when we spend too much time
  gazing into heaven;
   remind us to look at you on the level, in the loving eyes
    of our friends and family;
  in the pained and bewildered eyes of the hungry,
   the shell-shocked, the refugee;
  in the eyes of our comfortable but unsatisfied neighbour.
Ascended Jesus, you are here with us, and you are welcome.

Read Acts1:1-11; Ephesians 1:15-23; Luke 24:44-53; Psalm 47 or 93

Feet on earth,
eyes gazing up to heaven,
followers of Christ,
we cannot see Jesus or touch him.

We have glimpsed God's glory
and heard God's word
and we want to stay rooted to the spot,
holding on to the moment of truth.

But there is more to life than this....

God of truth,
help us to celebrate
your love,
your power
and your hope
at all times and in all places.

Take our feet onto new paths
where we tread with trust
because we walk with you.

Direct our eyes to people we never notice
who need your care
and your passion for justice.

Help us not to look to the skies
for our glorious inheritance
but to receive it
and to share it here
and now.

Acts 1:15-17, 21-26
Psalm 1
1 John 5:9-13
John 17:6-19

Mary's list

Challenged at a mission school organised by the Union of Welsh Independents to list the people in her community she would like to see in church with her, Mary Davies prayed for God's guidance and eventually prepared two lists. The first was of individuals her own age with whom she had attended Sunday school years before; the second was drawn from families who had loved ones buried in her church's graveyard. She began to approach those on her list and was soon asking a supporting minister to prepare some of them for church membership. After two years of her ongoing personal mission, her church has been transformed and revitalised. There is now a vibrant Sunday school and a significant Christian fellowship to which the community turns as a family support.

Pray with the Union of Welsh Independents (CWM Europe region).

Easter 7

Read Acts 1:15-17, 21-26; John 17:6-19

In Christ you call us
to follow.
You invite us to walk your way
that is unmapped
yet leads to joy;
you call us by name.
(pause)
God of the ages, **help us to follow**

In Christ you call us
to witness;
you give us your life
to share
and to proclaim,
you call us by name
(pause)
God of the ages, **help us to follow**

In Christ you call us
to learn.
You show us your truth
that never ends
and is always new.
You call us by name.
(pause)
God of the ages, **help us to follow**

In Christ you call us
to hope.
You offer us your love
to change us
and sustain us.
You call us by name.

God of the ages, **help us to follow.**

Seed of the Spirit

The Revd C Vanlalhruaia wrote from India to *Inside Out:*

Mizoram is a small hilly Indian state between Myanmar and Bangladesh. The Welsh Presbyterian missionaries came here to preach the gospel in 1894. Within a short period of time, practically all the Mizos became Christians.

By the grace of God, the Mizoram church has experienced frequent spiritual revivals. As a result, the seed for missionary work has been sown deeply in the hearts of the Christian youths. Despite the small population of Mizoram, the Presbyterian Church sponsors 940 missionaries. It also has three missionaries serving under CWM.

There are many youths who have come forward and offered themselves for missionary work. These youths are ready to go wherever the Lord sends them. They have a strong conviction about their call but have no outlet to fulfil it. Please do remember these dedicated youths who are saying, 'I am here, send me wherever you wish.'

Pentecost

Read   Ezekiel 37:1-14; Acts 2:1-21; John 15:26-27; 16:4b-15

Spirit of truth,
you dance through our world
marking paths of goodness and joy.

You leap into our midst,
waking us up and moving us on.

> Spirit of truth, **be our guide.**

You caress us in our brokenness,
holding us and healing us.

You irritate us in our complacency,
confounding us and challenging us.

> Spirit of truth, **be our guide.**

You ignite fires of passion
which burn for justice and peace.

You breathe winds of hope
to freshen deserts of despair.

> Spirit of truth, **be our guide.**

You come to us all.
You will dance for eternity.

One with the Creator,
gift of the Redeemer,
Holy Spirit, we welcome you!

15 June
Refugee Week

Isaiah 6:1-8
Psalm 29
Romans 8:12-17
John 3:1-17

At home in Newham

When a Brazilian family started attending a United Reformed Church in the Newham area of London, the other church members became increasingly aware of the problems faced by Latin American immigrants around them. Over 33,000 single asylum-seekers and 35,000 asylum-seeking families were living in Newham in January 2001 - more than in any other part of the UK apart from Kent, where Dover is the main port of entry. In the late 1990s the Newham churches, with help from the borough's leisure services departments and the Churches' Commission for Racial Justice, founded Breakthrough - a service which would enable Latin Americans to be at home in Newham. In its first year Breakthrough helped 100 people to gain access to welfare benefits, helped 80 with immigration issues, and dealt with 200 cases of need relating to language, housing, health, education, employment and leisure.

Asylum-seekers face long bureaucratic and judicial delays while they await recognition. One young woman fled Colombia with her children two years ago, leaving her husband, an active trade unionist, in hiding following death threats. In Newham her children, who miss their father very badly, have been ill and she has been burgled twice. Her benefits were stopped for two weeks while she waited for an appointment with the social services. But for her Breakthrough has been a constant support, 'like my second family,' and she helps out at the centre every week. Breakthrough's annual report quotes the biblical mandate to care for 'the widows, the orphans and the strangers within your gates'.

When our world is shaking and we have nowhere left to stand,
awesome God, you are our rock.
When our wisdom is shattered and we have to learn again,
awesome God, you are our truth.
When our worth is sinking and we feel enslaved,
awesome God, you are our home.

Now we need not be afraid, our guilt is gone.
Forgiving God, you are our friend.
Now we are not without hope, our failure is past.
Forgiving God, you are our life.
Now we will not be condemned, our Saviour is here.
Forgiving God, you are our peace.

Adopt us as your people and we will be your children of light.
Empowering God, love us.
Fill us with your Spirit and we will be your witnesses.
Empowering God, inspire us.
Send us on your mission and we will follow your way.
Empowering God, lead us.

Celebrating

The cradle of the Presbyterian Church of Wales is Coleg Trefeca, now a residential training and retreat centre serving all denominations in Wales and beyond. Coleg Trefeca is the birthplace of Howell Harris, a prominent leader of the evangelical Methodist movement in Wales in the 18th century. The year 2001 saw the celebration of 250 years since Harris knocked down his own small cottage, began to build the present historic building and set up a self-sufficient Christian community know as the Trefeca family (Teulu Trefeca). A bilingual musical show was written to mark the anniversary and performed by primary children from the local English-speaking and Welsh-speaking schools in a marquee in the College grounds - a unique opportunity to share with the local community the inspiration of a story which has shaped Christian history in Wales.

Pray with the Presbyterian Church of Wales (CWM Europe region).

Read   Job 38:1-11; Mark 4:35-41

Thank God,
> who was there when the stars sang
>> and the earth was formed;
> who was there when the sea was born
>> and the clouds clothed it;
> who was there when the wind whirled
>> and the storm broke.

Thanks be to God.

Thank God
> who is here calming our calamities
>> and delivering from distress;
> who is here stilling the storm
>> and promoting our peace;
> who is here questioning our qualms
>> and awakening our awe.

Thanks be to God.

Thank God,
> for those who are there amid hardships
>> and with us through sleepless nights;
> for those who are there with patience
>> and with us in genuine love;
> for those who are there offering powerful truth
>> and defence of honour.

Thanks be to God.   Amen

Away from crime

The Good News Centre in the squatter settlement of Kaugere, in Port Moresby, Papua New Guinea is ministering to young street people and has begun working with former convicts. Kaugere is notorious in Port Moresby for its high levels of crime and poverty. Many of those who come to the centre have been rejected by their relatives or have left their own villages to seek work in the city. United Church moderator Samson Lowa says, 'We see this as a place of rehabilitation, and this includes offering skills to the people who have come out of jail or who are drifting towards petty crime... We pray that through this God will bless the whole of Papua New Guinea.'

Pray with the United Church in Papua New Guinea (CWM Pacific region).

Read   Mark 5.21-43

A Psalm of Thanksgiving

God, I give thanks.
When I was down you lifted me.
At your touch the pain eased.
You spoke to me and gave me peace.
My faith and trust in you is justified.
God, I give thanks.

God, we give thanks,
even when we feel excluded from love,
when tears sting and hearts ache,
for your wish is our good, not suffering;
your purpose is our life, not death.
God, we give thanks.

God, all give thanks
when grieving becomes dancing,
when guilt turns to joy,
at the time healing comes,
when the day of release arrives.
God, all give thanks.

God, thanks be to you.
For your gifts of life and love
we would excel in love to you;
for your gifts of hope and healing
we would be generous with grace to others.
God, thanks be to you.

Ezekiel 2:1-5
Psalm 123
2 Corinthians 12:2-10
Mark 6:1-13

On the net

An internet cafe has been opened in Auckland by the
Congregational Union of New Zealand (CUNZ), with support from
the Council for World Mission, to increase the church's outreach
among young people. The idea came from CUNZ mission enabler
Bob Franklyn, who saw a similar church-run cafe while visiting
Taunton in England and told his own local church about it.
The cafe was initially open for two hours every other Friday
evening and offered two computers, games and food to its
customers. Shaila Barna, one of the young people from Three
Kings Congregational Church, Auckland, which runs the cafe,
said 'We're focusing mainly on teenagers, but anyone else who's
interested can come along.'

Pray with the Congregational Union of New Zealand (CWM Pacific region).

Read   Mark 6:1-13

You who are among us,

When we say …   then, remind us …

Who do you think you are?   'I cannot be honoured by you
                                    if you do not accept me.'

What could you possibly tell us? 'I cannot get through to you
                                    if you do not listen to me.'

Who gave you authority?   'I cannot be strong for you
                                    if you will not let me.

What could you do for us?   'I cannot heal you
                                    if you do not trust me.'

Who asked you to come?   'I cannot stay with you
                                    if you do not welcome me.'

**When you move among us
may we recognise you and welcome you
in female and male, in old and young, in friend or stranger.**

Radiant Christians

Myanmar is a beautiful country, full of surprises. Known for its radiant golden pagodas, it is also home to an equally radiant but less well-known Christian community. CWM's partners there, the Presbyterian Church of Myanmar, grew from the work of missionaries from the Presbyterian Church of Mizoram in north-east India, so it is truly the product of local mission. It is concerned to present the Christian message in the local languages and dialects of the people it serves across northern and western Myanmar, so its synods are organised not just geographically but by language area, seeking to demonstrate God's acceptance of all people by meeting them where they are with their own language and customs. In such a richly diverse country this recognition of difference is well received and is helping the church to demonstrate the breadth of God's love, giving new hope to people who otherwise had felt marginalised.

Pray with the Presbyterian Church of Myanmar (CWM South Asia region).

Holy God,
When our culture is measured
by your spirit level,
what bias will be revealed?
**Prepare us for the time of trial,
and seal us with your Holy Spirit.**

When our judgment is challenged
by legitimate authority
what integrity will we demonstrate?
**Prepare us for the time of trial,
and seal us with your Holy Spirit.**

When our fate is determined
by corrupt powers,
what reaction will be provoked?
**Prepare us for the time of trial,
and seal us with your Holy Spirit.**

When our faith is tested
by cosmic questions
what testimony will we declare?
**Prepare us for the time of trial,
and seal us with your Holy Spirit.**

When our love is demanded
by desperate needs,
what wonders will be celebrated?
**Prepare us for the time of trial,
and seal us with your Holy Spirit.**

New newspaper

The religious magazine it formerly published has been changed to a news and current affairs paper by the Kiribati Protestant Church (KPC). It will include religious news but bible teaching will be moved to another KPC publication. The church newspaper, called Mauri, was officially launched by Kiribati's Minister for communication, information and transport and is looking to build on its initial circulation of 1,200. It gives the Pacific island a third weekly newspaper - the others are owned by the government and by Kiribati's first president, Mr Yeremia Tab'ai.

Pray with the Kiribati Protestant Church (CWM Pacific region)

Pray for all Christians and churches working in the media of publishing, broadcasting and the internet, that they maybe able to maintain gospel values in their work and may find ways of communicating those values in their own communities. Pray for all whose freedom, livelihood, and even life itself may be threatened by their proclamation of the good news, that they will find the strength of Jesus Christ in honesty, bravery and vision. Pray for their families, and for the support of their churches.
Pray for Feed the Minds, an ecumenical Christian agency based in Britain, which supports communications around the world with money, equipment and training.

Read   **Psalm 23, Mark 6:30-34, 53-56; Ephesians 2:11-22**

Jesus saw the crowd and had compassion....
They were like sheep without a shepherd.

Incarnate God,

amidst the hustle and bustle of life you
meet us, and invite us to follow you.

Temper our exclusive ways;
Heal our desire to stand alone;
Encourage us to be one.

Give us a new understanding.
Orchestrate our lives, that through
Oneness and not obligation or habit, we seek to
Draw closer to you and to each other.

Sanctified by the death of Christ,
Held in the love of Christ,
Enable us to welcome the stranger
Presented by Christ as our brother or sister.
Holy and loving God,
Engage us in the jigsaw of the Kingdom,
Responsive, resting, re-united;
Delivered from desolation.

The Lord is my shepherd, I shall not want;
He leads me beside still waters;
He restores my soul...
...I shall dwell in the house of the Lord.

2 Kings 4:42-44
Psalm 145:10-18
Ephesians 3:14-21
John 6:1-21

For youth

To overcome a shortage of ministers and trained youth leaders, Nauru Congregational Church has embarked on a training initiative with the help of a CWM grant. The grant is being used to build an arts and craft centre which will include a classroom devoted to leadership training. The room will contain computers for training and musical equipment, to help young people to contribute more to worship.

Pray with Nauru Congregational Church (CWM Pacific region).

Read   John 6:1-21; Ephesians 3:14-21

Millions starve as famine strikes their land,
Dust-ridden, dry land where seeds perish
and hungry children cry for food.

Jesus took bread...gave thanks... and shared.

Millions die as dirty water spreads disease:
a slow, painful death
respecting neither young nor old.

Jesus took bread...gave thanks... and shared.

Millions suffer as they live on the streets:
no home, no family, no security,
cardboard and plastic for a bed.

Jesus took bread...gave thanks... and shared.

In the face of such despair how can we help?
What good is my loaf and fish?

Jesus took bread...gave thanks... and shared.

Almighty God, dispel our doubt.
Through your power within us deepen our trust
that we may believe in the miracle of life
that is Christ in the world:
feeding the hungry, saving the thirsty, loving the homeless.

Jesus took bread...gave thanks... and shared.
Help us take bread, give thanks and share.

Exodus 16:2-4, 9-15
Psalm 78:23-29
Ephesians 4:1-16
John 6:24-35

Bread of Life

We gnaw, gobble, gorge, graze, gulp and guzzle
without glimpsing the want in the eyes of others;
consuming God's providence as good fortune or fate.
We fail to recognise self-indulgence
as we hoard, accumulate and lay up reserves.
Craving saps our vitality, vigour and vivacity for God.
Called to care for the earth,
we live concurrently and not collectively;
lusting after and losing our heart to the world;
valuing and worshipping that which will perish,
and limiting our life.

Almighty God, we cry out from the desert,
save us from our gluttony.
Help us to share your world,
to live side by side with all your people,
the cooperative of the Kingdom.
Help us to discern the way of Christ;
to seek salvation through the everlasting sustenance,
the bread of life.
Taking only what we need,
may we cherish each opportunity to be together,
fuelled by love and driven by devotion.
For truly you are the bread of life
and through you no-one need ever hunger.

We step out eager, full of hope;
here is our deliverance, our liberation;
and then we find another locked door.
Even then, you are there with the key.
You will open the door
and we can step through, safe in your care.

Sustaining God, we see the door but fail to step through,
preferring instead to store perishable food.
Self-created independence over trust in God.

Manna for the Israelites:
a Saviour for the world:
bread of heaven, given for all.

We are hungry yet we fail to eat the bread of life.
We are captive yet we fail to take the road to freedom.

Almighty God, deliver us from ourselves
into the joy and care of Jesus.
Let us feast on your bread and believe in your love;
a love greater than our understanding,
a love which lasts forever.

Manna for the Israelites:
a Saviour for the world:
bread of heaven, given for all.

Rehabilitation

The United Church in the Solomon Islands has taken part in the first rehabilitation seminar ever to be held in the Pacific country's prisons. The Revd Mareta Tahu led a two-day seminar for the inmates of Rove Maximum Prison with the theme Behavioural Modification, Rehabilitation and Management. His team taught prisoners the bible, health issues and social skills. Prisoners said that their morale had been lifted and they had experienced God's comfort through the visitors. Prison superintendent George Tonafale is looking forward to the continuation of the seminars.

Pray with the United Church in the Solomon Islands (CWM Pacific region).

Read   1 Kings 19:4-8; John 6:41-51

Almighty God you love us and you trust us,
drawing us gently towards you, step by step, moment by moment,
experience, encounter, engagement.

Yet we fail to see and feel you.
We are blinded by our own expectations,
containing you within our own experience.
Expecting the encounter to be familiar,
we reject the touch of a stranger;
we turn aside from the unfamiliar face
and miss the look of your love.

'I have come down from heaven'.
How can this be?

We know your sort!
We don't want you here!
You have nothing to give me!
Rejecting your children, we reject you.
We fail to see the angel sent to deliver your message.

Open our eyes to see the messenger.
Open our ears to hear your words.
Open our hearts to love as you love,
without prejudice, bitterness, pride or expectation;
simply loving as Christ loves,
welcoming all,
caring for all,
sharing with all the bread of life;
touched by angels,
touching angels,
living life in all its fullness,
eager and ready for the unexpected
sent in the name of Christ.

Tuvalu's watery destiny

The highest point on Tuvalu is just four metres above sea level. Fifty hectares of this tiny Pacific nation of 10,500 people disappeared into the sea during cyclones Gavin, Hina and Kelly in 1997. Five years on, after watching many such troubling changes on its nine inhabited islands, the government of Tuvalu has concluded that it is destined to become the first nation sunk by global warming. A deal has been struck with New Zealand, in which 74 Tuvaluans will be resettled there each year, starting now.

The prospect of rising seas or tropical storms engulfing their nation has left Tuvalu's deeply Christian people grappling with a fear of the ocean, a belief that God won't flood their land and anxiety that their culture might not survive transplantation to a developed Western nation such as New Zealand.

More than 97per cent of Tuvaluans are Christians and there is a strong belief in the story of Noah's Ark, and God's covenant that he will not flood the earth again. The Revd Pitoi Etuati, who ministers in a 1,000-strong congregation, understands, unlike many of his fellow pastors, that the sea will eventually cover the islands 'if not in our time, then in the future'.

'It might be God's ways to inform us that there will be a time when this island sinks, so we have to push our government to make arrangements so we can be refugees, if not in our time then for the coming generation.'

Patrick Barkham
in The Guardian, 16 February 2002

Pray with Ekalesia Kelisiano Tuvalu (CWM Pacific region).

Read **Proverbs 9:1-6; John 6:51-58; Ephesians 5:15-20**

Sing to the Lord a new song
for wisdom has come amongst us,
teaching and showing the ways of God.

Jesus Christ is alive in us.
The Spirit of God rests with us,
filling us with hope,
and we sing to the Lord a new song.

We have turned aside from the simple ways of the world
and feasted upon the bread and wine of wisdom.
No longer are we ignorant,
now we grow in Christ.
We see for Christ,
we feel for Christ,
we love for Christ,
we are part of the body of Christ.

We share in the knowledge and experience of the body,
we learn from one another.
No longer living for self,
we live for Christ,
bringing hope to others,
feeding others,
loving others,
we are part of the Kingdom of God.

Jesus Christ is alive in us.
The Spirit of God rests with us
and we sing a song of praise and thanksgiving
in the name of Christ our Saviour.

Samoa's Bible

'I have a dream of bringing the Samoan Bible back home to Samoa,' says the Revd Tonu Peleseuma, manager of Malua Printing, the printing-house of the Congregational Christian Church in Samoa. It has sometimes been difficult to get supplies of the Samoan Bible, which has been printed in Korea, and the Church wants to encourage the use of a recently-approved contemporary Bible version, rather than the traditional version which continues to be supplied to Mormon and Seventh Day Adventist congregations. The Congregational Church is working with the Bible Society in New Zealand on plans to make it possible for Malua Printing to publish the new version. The press has been a success story for the Church, attracting jobs throughout Samoa and the Pacific by its quality and punctuality.

*Pray with the Congregational Christian Church in Samoa
(CWM Pacific region).*

Read   John 6:56-69

Christ Jesus, Son of God,
risen Lord,
earth cries out and you answer,
teaching us with sign and symbol,
opening God's word in patient parable.
Yet relying on ourselves
we reject you.
To whom can we go?
  You have the words of eternal life.

Risen Lord,
earth cries out deliver us
and you say, 'eat with me,'
and we eat of you,
bread and wine,
meekness and majesty,
enough for all, and still
we rely on ourselves.
To whom can we go?
  You have the words of eternal life.

Saving God,
patient and probing,
you unsettle us with questions;
searching and challenging,
taking us beyond reason to belief,
asking only faith.
In faith we come,
not because we know
but because we dare to dream,
earth-shattering dreams
of a kingdom of love in which
we rely on you.
To whom can we go?
  You have the words of eternal life.
    and in you we trust.   Amen

Self-sustaining

People in Madagascar who contract leprosy are shunned and ill-treated even by their own families, who fear, wrongly, that the disease is hereditary. Those who manage to get to hospitals such as Manankavaly, which has a leprosy mission, can be quickly cured but may still be rejected in their own villages. Since the late 1990s, a group of them have lived at Mahajery village, far from the towns, as part of the Madiova ('be clean') project, the brainchild of a young pastor of the Church of Jesus Christ in Madagascar. Mahajery is a planned agricultural village, created when former leprosy patients said they would like to earn their own living. Three years after its creation, the villagers are well on their way to being self-sustaining, growing rice, potatoes, cassava, beans and other vegetables and tending chickens and zebu oxen; and they have rediscovered their dignity as people.

Pray with the Church of Jesus Christ in Madagascar (CWM Africa region).

Read   Mark 7:6-8; James 1:21

My goodness – those pharisees!
How did you put up with them, Lord?
All those laws and ritual.
No true worship.

Not like us.
We've thrown out ritual.
Well, OK, we have the odd candle – but nothing more.
And no meaningless words –
*   though I must admit we did speed through the Lord's Prayer a bit today.*

But everyone lines up to thank the preacher.
'Good sermon today.'
'Helpful service – nice worship.'

But, through our smugness and self-congratulation, you ask –
what is worship?
*You tell us clearly that listening is not enough – we are called to **do**;*
to worship with every part of the life you have given us.

Forgive us, Lord, that we still miss the point:
    that we still find it easier to worship you with our words, rather than our
        bodies and hands;
    that, hearing your message, we still push it to the back of our minds
        and don't use it to guide our everyday living.

Thank you, Lord, that despite our short-sightedness, our ignorance and
our apathy,
    you do not write us off;
    you keep giving us more opportunities and another chance –
        another chance to discover what true worship is.

We pray, Lord, for vision and courage,
    that our lives may be living worship at every time and in every part.

Peace-brokers

When police clashed with gunmen, leaving 24 people dead in West Kingston, Jamaica, in July 2001, two church groups led peace marches into the area. As Jamaica's political gangs turn to the drugs trade and fight turf-wars fuelled by desperate poverty in the inner city, community leaders are looking to the Church to broker peace. St John's church in Hannah Town, alongside other churches, has for years carried on a quiet process of education - especially among young Jamaican men - and ministry, in the hope that the guns will stop one day, and that Jamaica's children will escape the war.

'It's hard to soar like an eagle if you hang around with chickens and buzzards all the time' - seen on a handwritten poster on a Kingston classroom wall by the URC members who visited Jamaica in 2001.

Pray with the United Church in Jamaica and the Cayman Islands (CWM Caribbean region).

Read   Isaiah 35:4-7a

People were overwhelmed with amazement. (Mark 7: 37, NIV)

Amazing God, you want to do more for us than we have dared to ask.
Your love has no ends, and knows no boundaries.

You want to give us life in all its fullness and wonder.
You see our limited understanding of your beauty,
    our failure to recognise your power and glory throughout creation
    and you send your life-giving Spirit to transform and to guide us.
You open our eyes afresh to the wonders of your love
    and you turn our wilderness existence into a Christ-affirming life.

Thanks be to you, amazing and loving God.

Amazing God, you want to give us wholeness of being.
You see our bodily and mental frailties,
    our aching limbs and teeming brains,
    and you stretch out your compassionate hands to heal us.
You give us strength beyond our expectations,
    a strength sufficient for the task you have entrusted to us.

Thanks be to you, amazing and loving God.

Amazing God, you want to give us your everlasting peace.
You see our confused and whirling minds,
    the worries and doubts we conjure up,
    and you send your enveloping love to release us and to renew us.
You gently blow away our fears
    and replace them with the certainty of your presence;
    the one God, the God who is with us now
    and who will be for evermore.

Thanks be to you, amazing and loving God.

14 September
Racial Justice Sunday

Isaiah 50:4-9a
Psalm 116:1-9
James 3:1-12
Mark 8:27-38

In the forest

Early missionaries in Guyana ministered principally to Africans who had been deported to the central American country and exploited there, and most congregations of the Guyana Congregational Union (GCU) are of mainly African descent. Now the Church is reaching out to the country's Amerindian people through a mission station and plans for social development.

An effective ministry to Amerindians in the Berbice River area was begun by the Revd Pat Matthews, himself of Amerindian descent, nearly 70 years ago, but access to Amerindian communities is difficult because many are deep within the rain-forest. The GCU has now undertaken a programme to provide health care, food and clothing for them, and is also using radio and television to raise awareness of the threat to the rain-forest from mining companies digging for gold and diamonds. Large areas of forest on Amerindians' ancestral land have been ripped down. 'We have a Christian responsibility to care for our land,' says GCU General Secretary Glen Johnson.

Pray with the Guyana Congregational Union (CWM Caribbean region).

Read   **Mark 8:27-33**

How difficult to get our words right! Perhaps, like Peter, there are occasions when we recognise that Jesus is the Christ, the Son of God, but then say or do something that denies the inevitability of what that means.

Again, in the quietness of our prayer time, we choose our words with care – but then, in the rough and tumble of our daily life, we let slip the angry retort, the ill-chosen words, that hurt or harm. 'Out of the same mouth comes praise and cursing.' (James 3:10)

Lord God,
words are such powerful tools;
they can praise or they can curse,
they can inspire or humiliate,
encourage or belittle.

Teach us, we pray, to use our words wisely –
        to praise your name and tell of your glory,
        to bring joy and hope to other people,
        to guide our children with love,
        to build up relationships.

And when we use words impetuously or harmfully,
        give us the grace to admit our error
        and to seek to build bridges of reconciliation.

Training ground

It is increasingly evident that theological and ministerial training within CWM member churches is in crisis, CWM general secretary the Revd Dr Desmond van der Water has told the Council's executive committee. In South Africa almost all the universities have cut their theological faculties since the end of apartheid and those faculties which do survive, with difficulty, are struggling. He urged CWM to identify institutions where training can take place, such as the Institute for Theological and Leadership Development of the United Church in Jamaica and the Cayman Islands.

Read   James 4:7-8a

Come near to God and he will come near to you.
Dismantle the barriers that stop you from seeing him.
If you have quarrelled, seek true reconciliation.
If there is self-centred anger in you, open yourself to God's
redeeming love.
If worries are distracting you, lay them in trust at Christ's feet.
If, in the hurly-burly of life, you have forgotten God, sit quietly and
make time to find him.

(pause)   **Come near to God, and he will come near to you.**

Put the ways and woes of the world to one side for a moment and
come near to God.
Recognise God's presence in your life –
in the joy you knew when seeing a newborn baby, an autumn sunset,
flowers blooming in the last of their summer glory;
in the beaming smile you saw on a child with something to tell you.

(pause)   **Come near to God, and he will come near to you.**

Recognise God's presence in your life –
in the time you gave to someone who needed your time;
in the words you spoke to someone who needed your words; in the
hand you stretched out to someone who needed your hand.
You are not far from God. Come nearer still.

(pause)   **Come near to God, and he will come near to you.**

Come nearer to God
         for as you come closer, you will know his presence,
         not far away, not even close by,
         but in you, in your very being.
You will know his peace, his love, his strength. And they will be yours.
Come near to God. He is near to you.

Growth

An extraordinary expansion of Christianity in China has been little appreciated in the West, says Caroline Fielder, China coordinator for the Churches Commission on Mission (in Britain and Ireland). The Church in China has grown from three million Roman Catholics and 700,000 Protestants when Communists came to power in 1949 to an estimated six million Catholics and 17 million Protestants today. 'For the first time,' she says, 'the churches are being seen [by the authorities] as part of the social vision for China.' But continued official exclusion of Christians belonging to the unregistered churches is still a grave concern and in some places arrests and harassment of priests and church members continues.

Read   **Numbers 11:10-11**

Moses was at the end of his tether.
He prayed in anger – blaming God for his current predicament.
But still he prayed.
He did not understand – but his faith that God was there did not waver.
And God answered his prayer.

It's easy to blame you, Lord, when things go wrong;
easy because we want to blame someone,
and easy to pick on you because you're always there.

It's easy to doubt you at times of crisis.
Easy because, despite what we say, we want an easy life,
and we tailor our faith to you providing us with an easy passage.
When things go wrong, they do not fit into the pattern we have drawn.

But at those times, at those black points in our life,
strengthen our faith, and help us to trust where we cannot understand.

When we see or experience tragedy,
when people say 'why did God let this happen?',
strengthen our faith, and help us to trust where we cannot understand.

When people cry out in pain, and others say 'where is God?',
strengthen our faith, and help us to trust where we cannot understand.

Our faith can be so fragile –
built slowly over the years as we seek to understand your way;
our uncertainties often remaining as uncertainties
but trying to trust where we cannot see.
Strengthen our faith, Lord,
so that crises do not make a mockery of what we have professed.

In those times, Lord, give us the grace to keep praying
and to rediscover our faith in your eternal goodness.

Genesis 2:18-24
Psalm 8
Hebrews 1:1-4; 2:5-12
Mark 10:2-16

New sight

Annual eye camps at Bollobhur hospital, Bangladesh, supported by CWM through missionary Gillian Rose, are curing hundreds of patients with cataracts. A team of specialists from the Bangladesh National Society for the Blind hospital near Khula performs over a hundred operations at the one-day camp, with volunteers from the local Church of Bangladesh congregation lifting patients on and off the operating tables and carrying them back to their places by stretcher. As the patients recover from the operation the volunteers lead a time of worship together. They are completely surrounded by a sea of faces, some bandaged, some veiled, as patients and relatives gather round to hear them sing and play. Muslims, Hindus and Christians hear together the gospel message of love, peace and harmony, says Gillian. A week later the patients, now able to see, receive their discharge slips and eye-drops and make their way back to their homes.

Pray with the Church of Bangladesh (CWM South Asia region).

Read Genesis 2:18-24; Mark 10:2-16

Lord, we got it all wrong.
You showed us your creation and let us make our mark on it.
You gave us a partner in love and work, who became our partner
in crime.
Making our mark turned stewardship into exploitation.
But you go on showing us your creation
and treating us with the respect we do not deserve. *(Silence)*

Lord, have mercy, and restore our respect for your creation.

You made us a little lower than the angels,
but we built barriers.
And then you sent your Son
to come this side of the angels
and to be the way to the other side. *(Silence)*

Lord, have mercy, and restore our respect for your creation.

'Love God with your whole heart and love your neighbour as yourself.'
'Treat your partner with respect: become one flesh.'
Welcome the birth of demanding children who sing God's praise
and receive God's presence:
that is how to start the restoration of respect. *(Silence)*

Lord, have mercy, and restore our respect for your creation.

If we respect our partners, our children, your creation;
If we love and respect them and you,
as you, despite everything, love and respect us …
Cost what it may – cost what it did,
then we may see your glory
in ourselves, in creation, in your Son. *(Silence)*

Lord, show us your love, and restore us.

12 October
Week of Prayer for World Peace

Amos 5:6-7, 10-15
Psalm 90:12-17
Hebrews 4:12-16
Mark 10:17-31

Pray for peacekeepers

Local churches in the Netherlands have been urged to give more pastoral care to military personnel who are sent abroad and to their families, and to make intercessory prayer for them in church services. The call followed a discussion on humanitarian intervention by Netherlands troops intended to end mass violations of human rights. An official report on the Srebrenica massacre of 1995, when Bosnian Serb forces executed several thousand Muslim men and boys in the Bosnian enclave, which was under the protection of Dutch United Nations peacekeepers, was the starting-point of the discussion. The report led to the resignation of the Dutch government in April 2002.

The discussion took place at a meeting of the three synods of the Uniting Protestant Churches in the Netherlands and was reported to local congregations. The meeting rejected a proposal to decide only on the pastoral issues and leave the basic discussion on humanitarian intervention to the political parties. Some 50,000 Dutch nationals - military and civilian - have been involved in peacekeeping operations abroad in the last ten years.

Pray for peacekeeping forces, including those of the United Nations, often serving in difficult and perplexing situations. Pray for the combatants in the world's wars asking that governments and policymakers may seek peaceful solutions to national and international disputes.

Read   **Psalm 90:12-17; Mark 10:17-31**

I want to be happy; I want to live.
I am grateful for what I have,
I thank you for it
but I don't want to give it up.

Yes, I want others to be happy, too.
I don't want them to be exploited;
I don't want them to be poor, or starving or sick.
Must I give up what I have?

I am enthusiastic,
I want to follow,
I'd like to bring with me my wealth, my talents, my family, my friends.
Must I give them up?

I've lived a reasonably good life;
I've won honour and respect from people;
I'm thought of as a good religious person.
Must I give that up?

Lord, it pierces my heart to be torn like this.
I feel the sword in my bones
Much more than I feel the sorrows of others;
Much more than I feel your sorrow.

Do I deserve the wrath of God?
Do I deserve to go away sorrowing?
It is hard to give up what I have;
It is hard for rich me to enter the Kingdom.

Yet, perhaps, Lord …
what is impossible for me
is possible for you.

19 October
One World Week

Isaiah 53:4-12
Psalm 91:9-16
Hebrews 5:1-10
Mark 10:35-45

It's an amazing mystery!
Now, as never before - one world.
From out of space, a ball of white and blue,
yet alive with life - alive with people - one world.
From its surface
life and matter held in delicate balance - one world.
And humanity, with technical power to shape the world,
and with decisive responsibility
to use its resources in one world.
For the world is one.
People can be fed and free;
the homeless can have homes;
the sick can have health;
the hungry can be fed.
The vision is full of hope,
rejoice in it - accept it.
But there is a price to be paid,
a dependence to be recognised,
brothers and sisters to be acknowledged and loved.

Hadn't they learned anything, these disciples?
No wonder the others were angry that James and John
had gone behind their back,
even if they wished they had had the idea first.

We all want special favours.
We all feel we deserve special attention from God.
Being saved isn't enough for us,
even though we know the right forms of words
to pretend that it is.

The evidence was all there:
Jesus had told them often enough
that the privilege of the saved
was serving and suffering;
that the servant must suffer like the master,
to share the master's greatness
and drink the master's cup
only to find that privilege does not follow as of right.

They hadn't learned,
and we find it hard to learn,
despite all the evidence of scripture
and the example of the saints.

Lord, though you suffer fools like us gladly,
help us to know that we have no claims,
that to follow you means suffering and service,
and that any honour is not to be grasped,
any reward not to be presumed upon.

Lord, have mercy upon our easy presumptions
and give us grace in our serving.

26 October
Bible Sunday

Jeremiah 31:7-9
Psalm 126
Hebrews 7:23-28
Mark 10:46-52

To talk with Christ

From the fourth century onwards the method of Bible reading known as *lectio divina*, 'divine reading', or, more loosely, 'reading with God in mind' was widely used... As one might expect, reading the scriptures in this mode cannot be hurried. We cannot enter into a conversation with Christ in a perfunctory and demanding manner... There are four movements in *lectio divina*: reading, meditation, prayer and contemplation. Archbishop Mariano Magrassi quotes Guigo's summary: 'reading, as it were, puts whole food into the mouth, meditation chews it and breaks it up, prayer extracts its flavour, contemplation is the sweetness itself which gladdens and refreshes.'

As we begin reading we choose a short passage from the Bible and read it slowly, verse by verse, taking our time before moving on... It is helpful often to read the verses slowly and aloud, waiting for a phrase to 'bite'. Meditation begins when we are struck by a word or phrase and chewing it over, sometimes repeating it over and over again, allow it to do its own work in us. 'Ruminating' was the way the Fathers described it, but I like Esther de Waal's image of rocking a baby backwards and forwards.

Prayer, the third stage, like conversation, will emerge naturally from the subject of the passage. Such prayer may take the form of thanksgiving, recollection, confession of sin or intercession for others. In time a sense of contemplation may come and the words of prayer will give way to sitting quietly in the presence of Christ. This stage is contemplation, sitting with Christ, not doing anything much, just being with him.

David Day
in 'Pearl Beyond Price'

Read Jeremiah 31:7-9; Mark 10:46-52

Blindness cured – rejoice!
Home restored – rejoice!
You are with us again – rejoice!

We think we see so clearly –
our universal blindness brings us sadness.

We feel at home
yet are restless, too,
and we are dissatisfied.

Bring us to sight
with clarity of vision
and readiness to serve

Show us our real home
and settle us there
in your presence.

We see afresh – rejoice!
We're home at last – rejoice!
Be with us for ever, Lord.
Rejoice with us!

Roadbuilders

Members of the Presbyterian Church of India co-ordinated the work of a bulldozer, 100 trucks and over 1,000 volunteers to rebuild the road to an isolated town in a single day. The 5 kilometer-long road between Rymbai and Ladrymbai had become so dilapidated that taxi-drivers and other commercial vehicles refused to use it. Many pregnant women delivered their babies before reaching the nearest health clinic. Under the supervision of pastors and church elders of the Rymbai Presbyterian Church, road workers and church volunteers worked from 8am to 6.30pm to compete the renovation, and were joined by people of other faiths in the community. 'The success of the work,' said the pastor of the Rymbai church, 'has prompted other churches to get more involved in social action.'

Pray with the Presbyterian Church of India (CWM South Asia region).

The Lord is our God.
But Lord, we still have many other gods:
wealth, social standing, power, authority.
All these and more crowd our minds
and distort our thoughts
leaving little room for you.

Week by week we make our offering of money,
but day by day we place more importance
on the material goods that money can buy.
We look for bargains,
ignoring the exploitation of fellow human beings
that makes our bargain possible:
the child labour, meagre wages, unsanitary living conditions.
Give us the perception to see beyond the bargain,
to use our money wisely
in loving our neighbour as ourselves.

Week by week we give of our time to the church,
but day by day we are concerned with how people see us:
the influence we have in groups and clubs,
our position at work,
our standing in the community.
Give us the sensitivity to see beyond our own importance,
to use our time and energy
for the good of all your people.

You, Lord, are our God.
We want to love you with all our heart, mind and strength.
Give us the wisdom not to be too selfish or afraid
to proclaim our faith in word and action.
Give us strength to shout,
The Lord is our God, the Lord alone!

9 November
Remembrance Sunday

1 Kings 17:8-16
Psalm 146
Hebrews 9:24-28
Mark 12:38-44

Girl child

The coordinator of the Church of South India's Girl Child campaign, Anne Rajkumar, has welcomed an Indian Supreme Court directive which will help combat the widespread practice of aborting female foetuses to give preference to male children. The Supreme Court has ordered state governments to confiscate unlicensed ultrasound scanning machines from health clinics, following claims that they were being used for sex determination tests. A 1994 law made such tests illegal, but thousands of clinics still offer them, with unlicensed machines, and recent studies show that in some regions over 99 per cent of aborted foetuses are female. Rajkumar warned that legislation would not itself solve the problem: 'Prejudice against the girl child is deep-rooted in society and we need to change it.' The Church of South India's Decade of the Girl Child aims to make church leaders aware of the extent of discrimination against girls and take the campaign to homes and villages throughout the 21 dioceses.

Pray with the Church of South India (CWM South Asia region).

Challenging God,
who sent Elijah to live in a foreign land
dependent on the generosity of others,
show us what we need for our journey
and what we need to leave behind.
Challenge us to travel,
wherever you send us,
in your name,
unencumbered by the shackles of earthly values.

Compassionate God,
who provided for the widow
when she thought she was going to die;
speak to us in our moments of need.
When we are lonely, anxious or depressed,
in illness or bereavement;
when life seems too much for us to bear,
give us faith to know that you are there.

Generous God,
like the one widow who gave all she had to feed Elijah
and the other who gave her few coins to further your work,
you provide for our every need.
You know what we require
and you give unstintingly.
Make us generous too:
with our money, time, energy
and, above all,
with our love.

16 November
Prisoners' Sunday

Daniel 12:1-3
Psalm 16
Hebrews 10:11-25
Mark 13:1-8

Witnesses

Progress made in bringing peace to Sri Lanka, where over 65,000 have died in an ethnic conflict since 1983, will bring huge relief to people like 42-year-old Mallika and her four children, who were forced by the conflict to move home eight times in the past 10 years.

Their last home during the struggle between the Sri Lankan army and the rebel Liberation Tigers of Tamil Eelam was in a refugee camp outside the fighting zone supported by Jaffna Diocese of the Church of South India. Once a Hindu, Mallika and her family became Christians because of the constant support given to them by church social workers. While most of the affluent members of the diocese emigrated to Australia, Europe and Canada because of the civil war, church membership soared from 5,000 in the 1970s to 25,000 - not due to proselytising, say church officers, but to the dedicated service of Christians among the displaced people, who came to the church for fellowship and security. It became 'the church of the poor'. The Jaffna diocese, which is Tamil and based in the north of Sri Lanka, has had the respect of both parties to the 2002 ceasefire, says Bishop S Jebanesan, because of its courage and integrity.

Pray with Jaffna diocese of the Church of South India
(CWM South Asia region).

Read Hebrews 10:11-25; Mark 13:1-8

Thank you God for the gift of your Son.
Thank you that throughout his life he showed us how to love;
how to care for the poor, downtrodden and marginalised;
how to welcome the despised and the outcast;
how to cherish the weak.
Thank you that by his death
we are able to live in that love.

There are times when our faith is shaken and fragile:
when wars, terrorism and civil unrest shatter lives;
when drought and famine leave people weak and dying;
when earthquakes, rising seas, hurricanes threaten whole communities;
when death or illness claim a loved one's life.

In these times of doubt
strengthen us to hold fast to our faith
and find your love and power
through the deeds and actions of our neighbour.
Enable us, too, to be channels of your peace and love,
supporting, cherishing and challenging,
to bring your kingdom on earth.

Teen educators

UNAIDS figures have shown that more than ten per cent of the 34 million people in the world living with HIV and AIDS are in India. The Church of North India has stepped up its HIV/AIDS education as the virus gains pace, spreading its HIV awareness campaign to all its 26 dioceses, which cover two-thirds of India. The Church has trained 3,000 school students aged 15 to 18 in New Delhi, the capital, to become 'AIDS teen peer educators', who spread the message on how to prevent AIDS. Some of their invitations come from non-Christian schools.

Pray with the Church of North India (CWM South Asia region).

Read   Psalm 93; Revelation 1:4b-8; Daniel 7: 9-10, 13-14

All-powerful God,
Alpha and Omega,
you reign with majesty and authority over your people.
You are mighty beyond our imaginings:
hotter than the hottest fire,
brighter than the brightest flame.
Mountains and oceans reverberate with your greatness,
rivers and plains are alive with your presence,
and we, your people, praise you.

You gave glory and power to your son, Jesus,
that we might see you in human form;
that we might glimpse your kingdom
and hear your truth.
Through his sacrifice on the cross
we are freed from our sins
and made your people.

Alpha and Omega,
God who is, who was and who is to come,
We praise you.

Acknowledgements

Prayers on right hand pages in this Handbook are by the following authors:
Brian Hudson - prayers dated 1 to 25 December and 31 August to 28 September
Terry Oakley - prayers dated 29 December to 26 January and 15 June to 13 July
Rachel Poolman - prayers dated 2 February to 2 March and 18 May to 8 June
Moira Rose - prayers dated 5 March to 6 April and 2 to 23 November
Alan Sayles - prayers dated 13 to 19 April and 5 to 26 October
Heather Whyte - prayers dated 20 April to 11 May and 20 July to 24 August

Meditations on left hand pages on 20, 27 April and 4 May are by Heather
Whyte, as is 'Bread of life' on 3 August. 'Struggling to learn' on 16 February
is excerpted from *Mansfield College Record* and used by kind permission of
Dr Tony Lemon. 'Rwanda's refugees' on 5 March is extracted from *Hope for
Rwanda* by André Sibomana, Pluto Press Ltd, London, 1999, used by
permission. The prayer on 18 May is from the resources for Christian Aid
Week 2002. 'Tuvalu's watery destiny' on 17 August is excerpted from *Tuvalu*
© Patrick Barkham, *The Guardian*, 16 Feb 2002. 'It's an amazing mystery'
on 19 October is from *Prayers and Meditations* by Tony Jones, reprinted by
permission of Christian Aid. 'To talk with Christ' on 26 October is taken from
Pearl Beyond Price: the attractive Jesus by David Day © 2001, published
by Fount/Harper Collins, used by permission of Zondervan. Left hand page
material for Christmas Day, Holy Week (14 to 19 April), and 29 May is by
the editor.

The editor gratefully acknowledges prayer material on left hand pages from
CWM member church contributors and publications, including that on 16
March (by Neil Chappel) from *The Congregationalist*, and on 2 March (by
Andrew Bradstock) and 15 June (by David Lawrence) from *Reform*. Left hand
page material on 31 August, by Nick Sireau, used with permission, is from
issue no 28 of *Inside Out*, the CWM magazine. Other material is from
Ecumenical News International, Inside Out and from CWM Info, a free internet
news service; details from kenwyn@cwmission.org.uk. The CWM website at
www.cwmission.org.uk gives details of these and other resources, including
free feature articles.

The photo on 12 January is by Terry Oakley, and that on 13 April (of the parish
church of Mijas in Spain) by the editor. The cover photo is by Hugo Dowd, and
is used by kind permission.

The Prayer Handbook is serviced by Wendy Cooper of URC House staff, with
help from Brenda Guest, and prepared for the press by Sara Foyle. The editor
is grateful to them all.